Life on Other
Worlds

Life on Other Worlds

Ray Spangenburg and Kit Moser

Franklin Watts

A DIVISION OF SCHOLASTIC INC.
NEW YORK · TORONTO · LONDON · AUCKLAND
SYDNEY · MEXICO CITY · NEW DELHI · HONG KONG
DANBURY, CONNECTICUT

For JILL TARTER
and in memory of
CARL SAGAN *and* BARNEY OLIVER

Photographs © 2002: Corbis Images: 19, 35 (Bettmann), 9, 98 (Reuters NewMedia), 25; Museum Victoria: 38; NASA: 44 (Ames Research Center), 26 (JPL), 54 (JPL/Malin Space Science Systems), 46 (NSSDC), 50, 102 (US Geological Survey), 22, 30, 51, 58, 64, 91, 96, 104, 109; Photo Researchers, NY: 12, 93 (ESA/PLI/SPL), 2 (Tony & Daphne Hallas/SPL), 17 (LOC/Science Source), 84, 85 (John Mead/SPL), 14, 53 (NASA/JPL), 41, 78, 79 (David Parker/SPL), 43, 111 (Ronald Royer/SPL); SETI Institute/Seth Shostak: 69, 77; Stone/Getty Images/World Perspectives: cover.

The photograph on the cover shows the Lagoon Nebula. The photo opposite the title page is an optical image of star clouds and nebulae around the central region of the Milky Way.

Library of Congress Cataloging-in Publication Data

Spangenburg, Ray 1939–
Life on other worlds / Ray Spangenburg and Kit Moser.
p. cm.— (Out of this world)
Includes bibliographical references and index.
ISBN 0-531-11895-9 (lib. bdg.)   0-531-15566-8 (pbk.)
1. Life on other planets—Juvenile literature. [1. Life on other planets.]   I. Moser, Diane, 1944–II. Title.   III. Out of this world (Franklin Watts, Inc.)
QB54.S69 2002
576.8'39-dc21   2001017968

1 2 3 4 5 6 7 8 9 10 R 11 10 09 08 07 06 05 04 03 02

Acknowledgments

We would like to thank the numerous people who have contributed to *Life on Other Worlds*. First of all, special appreciation goes to our editor, Melissa Palestro, who carried this book to completion, and to Melissa Stewart, whose creativity and vision sparked the inception of this series. We would also like to thank Sam Storch, lecturer at the American Museum–Hayden Planetarium; Margaret W. Carruthers, planetary geologist, Oxford, England; and Richard Ash of Oxford University and the Natural History Museum in London, who reviewed part or all of the manuscript and made many perceptive and helpful suggestions. If any inaccuracies remain, the fault is ours, not theirs. Also, our thanks to astrobiologists Jill Tarter and Chris McKay for their fascinating conversations with us on this subject. Special appreciation to Edgar Brichta, Bob Dreizler, Ron Fredrickson, Diane Fronczek, Rudy Iwasko, Alvin F. Ludtke, Kenneth E. Nahigian, John Nappi, Patricia Nappi, Ruth Rezos, Pauline Sweezey, Glen Walker, and Ed Wood for participating in a roundtable discussion on some of the issues. Thanks as well to Tony Reichhardt and John Rhea, our editors at the former *Space World Magazine*, for starting us out on the fascinating journey we have taken during our years of writing about space.

Contents

Life as We Know It

Life is all around us on Earth. Our planet overflows with many kinds of living things—from lacy ferns to giant humpback whales; from tiny, one-celled amoebas to towering pines; and from vast plains of wheat to mighty rhinoceroses. Microscopic bacteria are so small that you cannot see them. Ants form colonies and organize work parties. Elephants trumpet their calls in the wilds of India and Africa. Colorful parrots and macaws live in the jungles of Brazil. Polar bears and caribou live in the cold tundra regions of Alaska and Canada.

In the past twenty years our view of the vast diversity of life on Earth has changed. Researchers have discovered living organisms collected around thermal vents deep beneath the ocean surface, far from the light of the Sun. Other extremophiles (organisms that live in

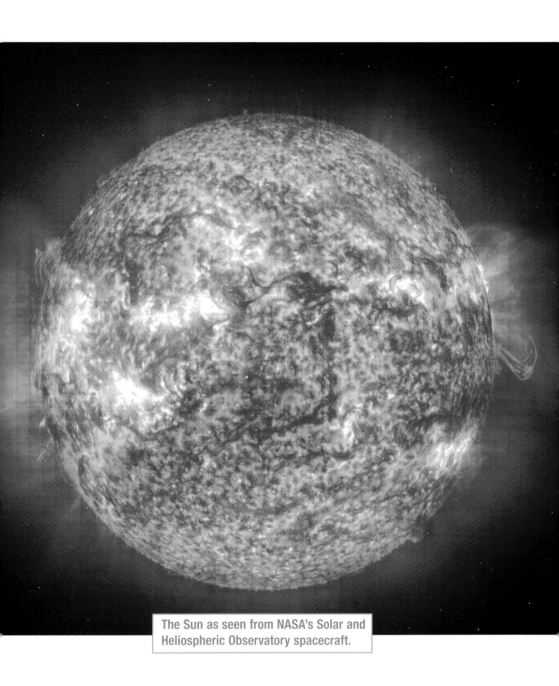

The Sun as seen from NASA's Solar and Heliospheric Observatory spacecraft.

extreme environments) have been found in Antarctica and other perpetually frozen locations. Since life began on Earth some 3.5 to 4.3 billion years ago, billions of different life-forms have developed. Now more than ever, scientists think life could also exist on some other world—maybe even on many other worlds—in the universe. Spacecraft exploring worlds within our solar system have found no proof of life nearby. However, many researchers think life in some form may exist elsewhere within our solar system, or that it might have once or will in the future. These *astrobiologists* are eager to explore worlds that may have oceans, such as Jupiter's moon Europa and Saturn's big moon, Titan.

Astrobiologists are actively looking for signs of life beyond our solar system. An astrobiologist is basically any scientist who either studies the origins and environments of life (on Earth or elsewhere) or focuses on searching for life beyond Earth. This special group includes scientists from various backgrounds, including chemistry, biology, geology, astrophysics, and astronomy. The field is especially exciting because people from many different fields are working together. They all bring their different expertise together to find out more about life and living things in the universe. Many astrobiologists think plants or animals may exist in another solar system surrounding another star far away. Perhaps many worlds like ours exist elsewhere in the universe. No one knows for certain, but the search is on!

In the pages that follow, you'll explore some of the many possibilities that researchers are considering. You'll find out about the scientific searches currently in progress. You'll also take a look at why scientists are certain that unidentified flying objects (UFOs) are not evidence of life on other worlds. Finally, you'll explore some of the questions raised by the possibility that we are not alone.

Chapter 1

Are We Alone?

The question "Are we alone?" has haunted the minds of humans for millennia. The question is huge and fascinating. Is Earth the only place where life has ever existed? Could life have been present elsewhere, too? Could living things be growing right now on another planet or moon in our solar system or somewhere else in the universe? What would they be like? Could life on Earth have begun somewhere else and floated through space to our planet? The biggest question of all is "Does *intelligent* life exist anywhere else in the universe?" Will we ever be able to find these beings if they do exist? Do we want to? And will we ever know the answers to all these questions?

Many science fiction writers explore these questions. In the motion picture *Mission to Mars* (2000), astronauts discover a "gateway" left

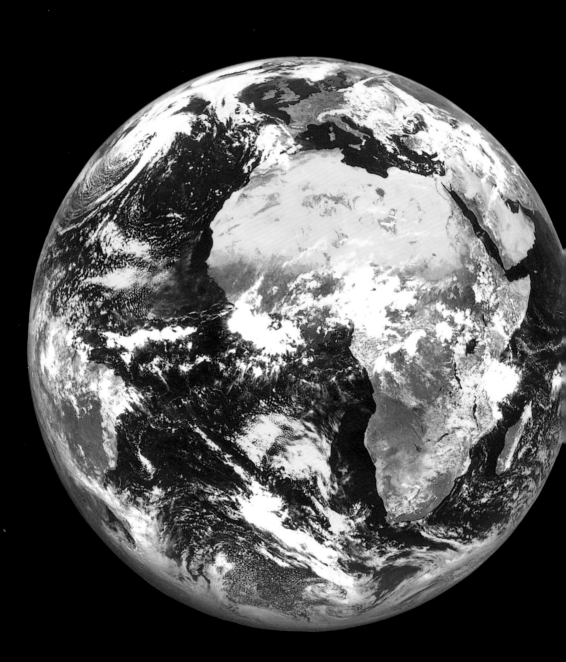

Meteosat satellite image of
Earth, showing Africa, Saudi
Arabia, and Europe.

behind by a Martian civilization that migrated to another *galaxy* long ago. In the motion picture *Contact* (1997), a scientist searching for signals from another intelligent civilization picks up a message from a faraway galaxy. *Independence Day* (1996) imagines an attack on earthlings by unfriendly aliens. Some films, such as *E.T.: The Extra-Terrestrial* (1982) and *Close Encounters of the Third Kind* (1977), paint friendlier visions of extraterrestrials (from the Latin words *extra-*, meaning "outside" or "beyond," and from *terra* meaning "Earth"). These films are based primarily on fantasy. They barely brush the surface of these enormous questions.

Some people think that we are not alone and that "they"—beings from an alien world—are here on Earth. In the mid-1950s people began to report what they believed to be "flying saucers"—saucer-shaped spaceships sent by a superior alien civilization from some far-away galactic empire. The U.S. government officially gave the name "unidentified flying objects" (UFOs) to these sightings. Since then, partly influenced by imaginative films and science fiction novels, UFO sightings have continued. Many people, from farmers to airline pilots, feel sure that they have seen spaceships hovering over Earth. Usually, these objects turn out to be commonplace—weather balloons, aircraft, and so on. No real evidence has ever been found that these UFOs are unearthly in any way. Sometimes, people eager to be written about in a newspaper or taped for the news have even faked photographs and other evidence. From what we now know about the solar system and the immense size of the universe, though, travel by UFOs across the great distances that exist would be almost impossible. No serious scientist is pursuing these extremely unlikely threads of possibility.

The Search

Today, though, a growing group of scientists is seriously investigating the possibility that life exists on other worlds. Their approach is completely different from science fiction, fantasy, or reports of "UFOs." These scientists are looking for solid evidence. They are working scientifically, using observations, physical laws, and reasoning. Right now, all they have are observations suggesting that life could exist elsewhere. Yet the evidence from these observations is piling up. In the

This photo of Jupiter's moon Europa was taken by the *Galileo* space craft.

coming years, new exploration may well provide some definite answers to at least some parts of the question "Are we alone?"

As the first years of the twenty-first century unfold, many scientists believe we stand on the brink, about to discover life elsewhere in the universe. They see several possible locations here in our own solar system where primitive forms of life either may exist now or may have existed in the past. Those places include Earth's neighboring planet Mars, Jupiter's moon Europa, and Saturn's moon Titan. Another group of researchers is actively searching the universe for Earthlike planets beyond our solar system—places that resemble Earth enough to make the existence of life a possibility. A third group is using high-tech equipment to "listen" for signals from intelligent life elsewhere in the universe.

All of these scientists are trying to answer that important question: "Are we alone?"

Views of the Ancients

This question of whether we are alone is a haunting, ancient one. Do other worlds teem with life? Are they populated by intelligent beings? As early as the sixth century B.C. (before the common era), the Greek thinker Anaximander (c. 610–545 B.C.) mentioned the idea that many worlds might exist. Two centuries later the famous Greek philosopher Epicurus (341–270 B.C.) saw our world as only a portion of the infinite universe. From that idea he reasoned that infinitely many worlds must exist in the universe. He also assumed that inhabitants lived on those worlds and that their populations must come in infinite variations. In Roman times the philosopher-poet Titus Lucretius Carus (c. 95–55 B.C.) also speculated that life existed in other parts of the cosmos. In his six-volume poem "On the Nature of Things" (56 B.C.) he wrote, "So we must realize that there are other worlds in other parts of the Universe."

These ideas were not part of mainstream thought, however. Other ancient philosophers thought human beings and their world were at the center of everything in every way. For the influential Greek philosophers Socrates (c. 469–399 B.C.), Plato (c. 428–348 B.C.), and Aristotle (384–322 B.C.), Earth was at the center of the universe. For the most part this anthropocentric, or human-centered, view dominated Western thought throughout the Middle Ages and Renaissance period in Europe. Christian church authorities, philosophers, and scientists all thought Earth was at the center of the universe and that all other celestial bodies *revolved* around it. Today, we know that this Earth-centered view is incorrect.

Humans: Awarded "Best in Class"?

Are human beings the "latest and greatest" of all living things on Earth? This idea lacks humility and bothers many people. However, humans have come a long way from the days when cave people hunted their prey with clubs. Since then humans have learned to control many aspects of their lives. They have studied the physical surroundings in which they live and have learned how to harness electricity, launch satellites, fly across oceans, and travel through space. Humans can talk to each other and write symbols that communicate ideas. They can communicate instantly between one side of the world and the other via e-mail, telephone, or fax. They can plan and build a space station—the International Space Station now orbiting Earth is proof. No other species on Earth can do all these things.

On the other hand, humans are physically very weak and are not really the "fittest" species around. Crocodiles, cockroaches, and bacteria have all survived since very ancient times—millions of years longer than humans have existed on Earth. They are the true survivors in the world and we humans are certainly not either the latest or greatest life-forms at all.

Of course, we humans are important to ourselves. So it is not surprising that many people thought humanity to be the best that the entire universe had to offer—the only intelligent life anywhere. They thought that Earth was unique and that no other planet like Earth could exist anywhere else. These people thought that Earth was specially designed for the development of life. They also felt that human beings were the most important and best-developed of all examples of life on Earth or anywhere else.

The geocentric (Earth-centered) view continued to have great influence on scientific and philosophical thought

Aristotle approved of the Earth-centered theory.

for many centuries. For thousands of years, people had watched the Sun, Moon, planets, and stars cross the sky. Celestial objects would appear each night in the east, travel to the west, and set—only to repeat the performance the next night. The ancient Greeks believed the Sun, planets, and stars all moved in perfect, harmonious circles around Earth. That's the way it looked to them, and because the concepts of harmony and perfection were important in ancient Greek philosophy, it all seemed to make sense. Aristotle also had great influence on philosophical thought for many centuries, and he had approved of the Earth-centered theory. A couple hundred years later, in A.D. 140, the philosopher/scientist Ptolemy of Alexandria, Egypt, made some adjustments so that this theory would still work after taking into account the recent observations made by astronomers.

Ptolemy did such a convincing job and the Earth-centered view was so popular that no one really challenged the idea of the geocentric universe until about 1,400 years later, in 1543. In that year a Polish scholar named Nicolaus Copernicus (1473–1543) published a new theory. Based on careful observations of the nighttime skies, Copernicus's theory concluded that the Sun—not Earth—is the center of our solar system. He saw that the planets, their moons, and all the other objects in the solar system were *orbiting* the Sun. Earth was not at the center after all. Just before Copernicus died, this revolutionary heliocentric (Sun-centered) idea was published in his book *On the Revolutions of the Heavenly Spheres*. This book set forth the idea that Earth was just one of several worlds that orbited the Sun, just as the other planets did.

A few years later, the Renaissance philosopher Giordano Bruno (1548–1600) stated his belief that Earth was not the center of the universe. He expanded on this idea in his book *On the Infinite Universe and Worlds* (1584), in which he wrote that "there is not merely one world, one Earth, one Sun, but as many worlds as we see bright lights around us." It was one of many ideas he held that angered the authorities of the Roman Catholic Church. Bruno was burned alive at the stake for his beliefs.

Copernicus's book continued to make waves in the scientific community. In about 1609 the great Italian astronomer Galileo Galilei (1564–1642) began using a telescope to observe the nighttime sky. (If you have an inexpensive backyard telescope, you have better equipment for observing the stars and planets than any scientist had even as

Galileo Galilei kept records of his observations of the night sky.

late as the seventeenth century.) As he looked through his telescope at the nighttime sky, he kept records. He soon noticed that the diameter of Mars seemed different in size depending upon the time of year he observed it. Venus also seemed to change size in the same way. Galileo realized that the planets were not really changing size. Mars and Venus must travel much closer to Earth at some times than at others. But how could that be if they circled Earth? Galileo realized that the pattern he was seeing was exactly what would happen if these planets traveled around the Sun. Sometimes they would be traveling far from Earth, on the other side of the Sun. Galileo recognized that Copernicus was right. As we now know, the Sun, planets, Moon, and stars do not really move across the skies every night, starting in the east and ending in the west. This movement is an illusion caused by the movement of the planet we're standing on as we observe. As Earth *rotates,* or turns, on its *axis* (an imaginary line through its poles), the objects in the sky seem to parade from horizon to horizon.

Galileo was excited and began to write and teach about what he had learned. However, the powerful Catholic Church held its position that the planets, Sun, and Moon all revolved around Earth. The Church ordered Galileo to stop teaching his ideas, but Galileo couldn't stop writing and talking about what he knew he had seen. In response to the scientist's disobedience, the Church tried him in 1633 and sentenced him to house arrest for the rest of his life.

Thanks to Copernicus and Galileo, however, a revolution had begun. By the middle of the seventeenth century, most of the world's astronomers agreed that the Sun and not Earth was at the center of our solar system. This was an important change. People began to understand that Earth was like other planets. It moved in the same way the other planets moved. The invention of the telescope also changed the way in which astronomers saw other planets. They could see the round disks of these spheres against the nighttime sky—the planets were no longer just tiny pinpoints of light. People began to realize that these objects were other "worlds," which were possibly a lot like our own.

Since that time many scientists have tried to find answers to more questions about these other worlds, such as: Are there other ways in which the other planets and Earth are similar? Are there other planetary systems in the universe? Could life exist elsewhere? And they began to wonder how the universe had been created.

The Beginning

How did all the objects around us get here? How did Earth get here? No one saw the universe begin. Yet, based on calculations and observations of the universe today, astronomers have a pretty good idea how it probably happened. They think that, at the beginning of time, an event known as the big bang occured. According to the big bang theory, everything in the universe—everything that we can see, touch, and detect or that can in any way affect us—was created by this event. Astronomers think this colossal explosion of something incredibly tiny and hot took place about 15 billion years ago. They believe that everything that exists today came initially from the helium and hydrogen that formed at the time of the big bang and that, from that moment, the universe began expanding and has been getting bigger ever since.

Some people wonder if there could be other universes or whether another universe existed before the big bang. No one really knows. Scientists have been able to discover evidence only of this universe and its history.

An artist's rendition of the Milky Way.

Birth of a Star

About 4.6 billion years ago in the *galaxy* we call the Milky Way, a cloud of gas and dust began to gather together. It was one of many such clouds in the Milky Way. Over time the cloud, or nebula, grew bigger and bigger. When it had become huge—trillions of miles across—it began to move slowly and then to rotate, or swirl. The rotating cloud center began to shrink inward upon itself because of *gravity*. As the *mass* in the central region became greater, this material began to contract even more. The amount of material at the center kept getting denser, and its gravitational pull kept getting stronger. So more material was attracted and pulled in, and the material at the center collapsed even more.

More *interstellar* gas and dust (from between the stars) fell into the center of the nebula, and its *density*, temperature, and pressure rose. At the dense center, hydrogen atoms began to break up into their atomic particles—protons and electrons. Protons (with a positive charge) usually repel other protons, but the extreme pressure and heat overcame that repelling force. *Nuclear fusion* began to take place—the joining of protons together. So hydrogen atoms (with one proton in the *nucleus*) turned into helium atoms (with two protons). The process released an enormous amount of energy. One result was the creation of even greater heat, which allowed even more energy to be released. What was once a huge cloud of dust and gas had become a colossal hydrogen bomb! At that moment, a *protostar* was born—just as many others had begun and were beginning throughout the galaxy and all the galaxies of the universe.

This particular star was our Sun. Of course, no one was there to see our Sun form. However, as long ago as 1755, a German physicist and philosopher named Immanuel Kant (1724–1804) came up with the idea that stars form from disks of gas and dust. No telescopes were powerful enough, though, to look at stars that were just forming. So no one had seen a disk of gas and dust of the kind Kant was describing. But the theory made sense, so scientists worked on Kant's initial idea—creating models, measuring *meteorites,* and looking for clues. One problem was determining how anyone could see the forming star at the center of a dark mass of swirling gases and dust. When astronomers began to point infrared telescopes on suspect areas, though—telescopes that could "see" temperature differences—they found that they could finally peer through the clouds. They began to find disks of gas and dust with infant stars beginning to form at their centers. More than two hundred years after Kant's work, in the 1980s, astronomers began to find conclusive evidence of stars forming within disks of gas and dust.

Rocks Around the Sun

Surrounding the infant star we call the Sun, the huge disk of hot gases and debris continued to swirl. The disk gradually began to cool and condense, forming solid masses. Most astronomers believe that the first solids were very small and eventually joined together to form bigger particles. Those joined together to form even bigger particles. Clumps of matter the size of houses or larger began to form. The bigger they became, the more gravitational attraction they had. They became attracted to each other and formed even larger bodies with *diameters* the size of asteroids. These were called *planetesimals.* This process is called *accretion.* Before long, accretion began to take place at a very rapid pace, as big objects began smashing into one another.

Eventually, larger and smaller masses formed, including what later became the nine planets of our solar system and their moons.

Some debris was not swept up into the planets and moons, though. These large chunks of rock and ice, which number in the trillions, make up the *asteroids* and *comets* that also orbit the Sun and are scattered throughout the solar system. Smaller chunks called meteoroids also form part of this system today. These are almost all bits that have broken off various moons, asteroids, and planets sometime since the formation of the solar system. A wide band of asteroids orbits in a region known as the *Asteroid Belt,* which is located between Mars and Jupiter. Others cross orbits with Mars and Earth. Still others even masquerade as moons. As was recently discovered, even asteroids

Comet Kohoutek was visible from Earth during the winter of 1973–74. It will not

When *Galileo* flew by Asteroid Ida in 1993, the spacecraft discovered Ida's tiny moon, Dactyl (right).

How big is the solar system? It takes light about one day to travel across the solar system. Our solar system is located in one of the billions of galaxies in the universe and is one of billions of stars in our home galaxy, the Milky Way. The Sun is located about 4.3 *light-years* from the nearest star, Proxima Centauri, and about 30,000 light-years from the center of our average-size galaxy. Light from the farthest galaxy we know of takes about 10 billion years to reach our telescopes.

What's a Light-Year?

Distances are so vast in the universe—and even in our own galaxy, the Milky Way—that scientists measure them in the time it takes for light to travel. The closest known star outside the solar system is 4.3 light-years away. That means that if you could travel at the speed of light it would take you four and one-third years to travel to Proxima Centauri. This measurement is very handy for talking about distant objects in the universe, since the distances are so enormous.

However, the voyage from star to star or galaxy to galaxy would take a spacecraft much longer than it would take light. According to Albert Einstein's special theory of relativity, no object can travel at the speed of light. As an object approaches the speed of light, its mass increases. Before it could reach the speed of light, all the energy in the universe wouldn't be enough to propel it. The object would become infinitely heavy, so it could never reach the speed of light.

This piece of information makes the presence of spacecraft from other worlds in Earth's neighborhood seem enormously unlikely. Human exploration has turned up no evidence of intelligent life elsewhere in our solar system, so the spacecraft would have to travel here from a world orbiting another star. It takes light four and one-third years to travel here from the nearest star, but no spacecraft could ever travel that quickly. The laws of physics apply to spacecraft from other worlds, too, and even an advanced spacecraft would have to travel much slower than light. Another problem comes from the fact that the closest star known to have planets orbiting it is very far away. Extraterrestrial travelers would have to travel for perhaps hundreds of years to reach our "pale blue dot" in the universe, as the late astronomer Carl Sagan (1934–96) liked to call our planet. This is one of the strongest arguments against the presence of "alien spaceships" in our solar system.

Looking for Real Life

We know that, on at least one planet in our solar system, a delicate process called life began. It was a process that flourished in the presence of water, an *atmosphere,* and mild temperatures. Today, human beings exist there, along with thousands of other life-forms. This planet, Earth, is the "third rock from the Sun," the third of the nine planets revolving around the star at the center of our solar system. Why did these conditions form here? What makes them good for living things? Where else should we look for life and what should we look for?

We may have to abandon the imaginary tales of visits from E.T. and Wookies that hang out in intergalactic sports bars. However, the real search for life in the universe is even more challenging and exciting than fiction, and no one knows what we will find.

The first task is to understand what life is and how it began here on Earth. The simplest thing to assume is that all life everywhere began in the same way. So if we can figure out how life began on Earth, we can assume how it began elsewhere. However, if life exists elsewhere, it may not have begun the same way. It may not rely on the same chemical processes as does life as we know it. And it probably doesn't come in the same shapes as life on Earth. (Think of the diverse forms of life that exist in your own backyard or take a trip to a zoo, and you'll see that, even on Earth, life comes in many, many forms.) However, scientists have learned that comparing Earth with other worlds is a great way to find out a lot about both our home and, perhaps, the home of some previously unknown life-forms.

Chapter 2

Life's Beginnings

So far, the only examples of life that we know anything about are the life-forms we have found on Earth. On our planet, living things require abundant water. Most scientists think that life on Earth began in our planet's vast oceans—possibly in shallow tide pools, underground, or near the heat of hydrothermal (hot-water) vents in the ocean floor. There, simple molecules moved about and were mixed together by the water's movements. Eventually, some of them joined in ways that formed *organic molecules*—substances containing carbon and hydrogen. Carbon, hydrogen, nitrogen, oxygen, and other elements attached themselves to each other and formed large molecules called

This photograph of Earth
was taken on April 16, 1972.

nucleotides. These large molecules became the building blocks of proteins that make up the tissue of organisms.

Most scientists think that life throughout the universe also would require the presence of water in order to exist. Many researchers think the best way to look for life on other worlds is to look for worlds that contain water.

What Is Life?

Before exploring how life may have begun, astrobiologists have found that they need to ask an even more fundamental question: What, exactly, is life? Even though scientists know a lot about living things and how they work, coming up with a definition of life itself is much more difficult. No one is really sure at the fundamental level what defines the difference between a living organism and a lifeless strand of molecules. Living things can usually perform certain activities, such as *metabolism* (chemical processes and reactions that take place within organisms, including the chemical transformation of food into energy), growth, reproduction, responsiveness, and adaptation. They also contain organic molecules that go through complex transformations. However, no one is sure how much of this description is a necessary part of life. When you step back from the details of life on our planet, what makes living things different from nonliving things in the most general, universal sense?

For example, can life be based on only the kinds of carbon molecules described as organic molecules? Does its development always require the presence of water? No one knows the answers to these questions. Even though carbon is by far the most versatile element when it comes to making a large variety of complex molecules, a few scientists think life might be able to develop using another central element—sulfur or silicon, for example. Some astrobiologists think another liquid, such as liquid methane, might work as an environment instead of water.

The History of Life on Earth

Vital Statistics

Era	How Long Ago (in millions of years)	Events in the Development of Earth's Life-Forms
CENOZOIC	0.0	Present time
	0.1	Modern humans appear
	2.4	Ice Age
	65–66.4	Mass extinction; death of the dinosaurs
MESOZOIC	141	First flowering plants appear
	195	Birds evolve from reptiles
	230	First dinosaurs and mammals appear
	245	Mesozoic Era begins
PALEOZOIC	280	Mass extinction
	340	First reptiles appear
	360	First insects appear
	370	First amphibians appear
	420	Plants begin to grow on land
	540	Paleozoic Era begins
PRECAMBRIAN	700	Simple multicellular organisms evolve
	2,100	Oldest *eukaryotic* fossils
	2,500	Oxygen buildup in the atmosphere
	3,500	Oldest *prokaryotic* fossils

How Did Life Begin?

One of the greatest scientific detective cases of all time is the mystery of how life began. It is a puzzle that has many parts. What were conditions like on Earth before life began? Early Earth was a far different place than it is today. What was it like during its formation? What was it like 3.5 to 4.3 billion years ago as life began to form? What molecules were present in the atmosphere and in what proportions? What were the original building blocks of life, and what processes took place?

How can we go about answering these questions without a time machine (there is no way to travel physically back in time)? Scientists have several methods for looking at the history of living things. First, they look at fossils—remnants of prehistoric living organisms that are usually embedded in layers of rock. Next, they perform experiments to simulate what happens under different environmental conditions. Then, they think hard about everything known about life, chemistry, and physics. Finally, they form *hypotheses.* If we ever do find life on another planet or moon, scientists will also study those life-forms carefully to find out more about what life is and how it might have begun.

Scientists who study meteorites have found organic molecules embedded in these ancient rocks from space. As meteorites travel through the solar system, some are attracted by our planet's gravity and fall through Earth's atmosphere to the surface. Sometimes people assume that the presence of organic molecules in meteorites shows that life may have come, ready-made, to Earth from space. However, the term "organic molecule" is misleading. As long ago as 1828, scientists figured out how to use inorganic molecules to produce so-called organic molecules, that is, they used molecules that were not found primarily in living organisms to synthesize organic molecules. In the process they showed that the same molecules could form in nature without the help of living things. The expression "organic molecules" refers to molecules made of carbon and usually hydrogen. However, *organic* does not mean that they are made by living things or that they are or were part of a living thing. Ready-made living things did not travel through space on meteorites. (Even if they did, scientists would ask how *that* life began!) So how *did* life begin?

In 1953 a graduate student named Stanley Lloyd Miller was working on an experiment in the biology laboratory at the University of Chicago. He did his work under the guidance of his mentor, Nobel laureate Harold Clayton Urey. Miller wanted to set up conditions to mimic what scientists then thought early Earth might have been like. He visualized early Earth as a place where great clouds of poisonous gases rolled across the turbulent surface of the planet's oceans and lightning flashed across the skies. Early in Earth's history, the protective ozone layer in the upper atmosphere had not yet have developed. So ultraviolet radiation from the Sun would have bombarded the surface of early Earth with great intensity.

Miller and Urey's question was this: What effect would the ultraviolet radiation have on the carbon-based molecules in the atmosphere? Miller and Urey thought that the gas molecules in the atmosphere would become excited and react with each other chemically. In the process they would combine into more complex organic molecules, such as *amino acids,* proteins, and nucleotides—all important building blocks necessary to most living organisms.

In order to test his hypothesis, Miller created an "atmosphere," made up of the gases he thought were present when life began, in a complex setup of tubes, beakers, and flasks. He introduced hydrogen,

This photo taken in May 1953 shows Stanley Miller working in the University of Chicago laboratory where he and Nobel Prize winner Dr. Harold Urey performed their landmark experiment.

methane, and ammonia above a beaker of sterilized water to simulate Earth's atmosphere hanging above the oceans. Then he stimulated the atmosphere with an electrical charge. After running the experiment for a week, he noticed that the water in the flask and in the trap below it had turned orange-red. Tests showed that the water contained concentrations of amino acids, a type of organic compound that often combines to form proteins. The experiment was repeated successfully many times by other researchers, producing all twenty of the amino acids required to form proteins. Miller and Urey had simulated the chemical conditions thought to be present in the environment of the young Earth. Their work showed that, under those conditions, organic compounds we know as the building blocks of life were able to form through completely ordinary, common processes. In a sense, they showed that organic substances could be the products of simpler inorganic precursors, given sufficient time for the reactions to occur. It was a landmark experiment.

Because their hypothesis was supported by experimentation, their view of how organic substances formed became a theory. Miller and Urey's theory has been further refined to include more recent ideas. Scientists now add that nucleotides would grow more and more complex until they developed into a nucleic acid, such as *deoxyribonucleic acid (DNA)*, that is capable of replicating, or copying, itself.

New information suggests that early Earth's atmosphere may not have contained the amounts of methane and ammonia that Miller and Urey thought were present. Miller and Urey thought early Earth's atmosphere resembled the makeup of the original disk of dust and gas that formed the Sun and the solar system. Today, though, researchers think many ammonia and methane molecules in early Earth's atmosphere may have been broken up by ultraviolet radiation from the Sun. Eventually, with many of these molecules broken up, the hydrogen held by them would have escaped from the atmosphere. So the atmosphere may have been different than it was in Stanley and Urey's model.

Others scientists disagree. These researchers point out that volcanoes or deep-sea vents could have belched additional quantities of methane from the center of the Earth into the atmosphere. Ammonia might also have come from deep-sea vents (even though it no longer does today). If so, these gases might have remained as a smoggy layer of the atmosphere, much as the moon Titan's methane atmosphere hangs above its surface. If this is the case, then Miller's experiment might still be a good imitation of Earth's early chemistry.

Hydrothermal Vents

Today, many researchers think the creation of organic molecules initially took place in water—perhaps in shallow tide pools warmed by the Sun. Since the recent discovery of hydrothermal vents on the ocean floor, other researchers think that life may have begun near these steamy regions, where outgassing from Earth's molten interior warmed the water and provided the ingredients for organic molecules to form. Many ecosystems exist in these regions today, where chemical energy (rather than solar energy) supports various life-forms. The raw materials and the energy to form the building blocks of life are there, as they were on the early Earth.

The question of where the necessary ingredients for life initially came from still remains unanswered, though. One popular theory favored by astrobiologist Carl Sagan proposes that organic molecules rained down onto Earth from space.

"Organic" Rain

As early as 1908, Swedish chemist Svante August Arrhenius (1859–1927) wrote a book called *Worlds in the Making,* in which he offered the hypothesis that Earth, along with other worlds throughout the universe, was seeded by living spores from outer space. Of course, this idea, known as panspermia, doesn't really solve the problem of where life originally came from. This theory did, however, lay the conceptual groundwork for a more recent idea that now seems to be the most likely explanation for how organic biochemistry may have begun on Earth.

Most scientists today think that life on Earth did begin here. But many now think that Earth's supply of organic materials did not form exclusively on Earth. Some of these organic materials may have come to Earth from elsewhere, carried in the constant "rain" of meteorites, comets, and dust grains that bombarded Earth in its early years. This idea may seem far-fetched, but evidence supports it. Researchers have discovered that a considerable variety of organic compounds can ride onboard all three of these kinds of objects. One meteorite class, called *carbonaceous chondrites,* can contain as much as 5 percent organic material. A meteorite found in Australia in 1969, known as the Murchison meteorite, contained more than seventy different amino acids. Eight of these amino acids number among the twenty basic ingredients for building proteins.

The thinking goes like this: When planets first began forming in the disk of dust and gas around our Sun, the solar system was a violent

The Murchison Meteorite fell in Australia in 1969. These pieces are presently at the Melbourne Museum, Museum Victoria.

place. Chunks of meteorites, asteroids, and planetesimals careened through space, smashed into one another, knocked one another out of orbit, and whizzed on to collide with other objects. Cataclysmic explosions and collisions made the place into a cosmic war zone—so much so that scientists sometimes call this period the great bombardment.

Today, meteorites streak through the atmosphere and smack into Earth's surface. On these meteorites, researchers have occasionally discovered complex organic molecules that date back nearly as far as the solar system's formation. The meteorites have been traveling around the solar system since they were first formed 4.5 billion years ago, and they have probably carried these molecules from the beginning. So even though organic molecules may not have existed on Earth when our planet first formed, these molecules certainly arrived onboard many of the meteorites that smashed into it in the first billion years of its existence. These organic molecules, scientists believe, were the raw materials from which life eventually formed.

Of course, the same kinds of meteorites were also bombarding all the other planets and their moons. So what made Earth special? Most scientists agree that the origin of life on Earth required the presence of an atmosphere, an ocean, and a stable crust, or solid surface. The rocky planets and moons were hot and molten in the beginning and cooled slowly, but some researchers interpret evidence that shows that Earth had an atmosphere, oceans, and a stable crust within the first 200 million years of its existence. Most estimates set the time of life's beginnings at about 3.5 billion years ago, the age of the oldest fossils ever found. But life may be a lot older than that. Recent studies using high-tech instruments show that stable amounts of water may have existed on Earth as long as 4.3 billion years ago.

Have you been wondering how all those organic molecules wound up in the chunks of rock whizzing around the solar system long before any life existed on Earth? If so, you're asking a good question!

Let's look for an answer in the Eagle Nebula, of which the *Hubble Space Telescope* has captured stunning images. Astronomers call this nebula M16 because that's the number it holds in the catalog of nebulae compiled by Charles Messier (1730–1817), a French astronomer with a passion for ordering things. This enormous mass of dust and gas has huge fingers that are sometimes referred to as star nurseries because of the number of protostars in them. This hot cloud is located about seven thousand light-years from Earth. It contains abundant supplies of raw materials—mostly hydrogen, the simplest of the elements, and a little helium. It is the scene of highly active star production, which is why it is so hot.

As you already know, when gravity causes regions of such a cloud to condense, a disk of gas and dust may form. Then the disk contracts further. As it collapses, its density and temperature increase until fusion is triggered and a star is born. Meanwhile, other objects may form around it, forming a planetary system composed of objects orbiting the star and one another.

Astronomers can detect the type of gases in a nebula like the Eagle easily, but what about the *composition* of its dust?

Researchers believe that this interstellar dust is formed from the nebula's gases. These materials did not form during the big bang, when the universe first began. However, over the billions of years since then, these heavier elements have formed within stars during the later stages of their life spans, when hydrogen fuel grows scarce and heavier elements begin to form from the fusion in the cores. At the end of the star's life *cycle,* it usually casts off its outer layers as a "planetary nebula," enriching the interstellar medium with elements such as carbon and oxygen. In the process, the heavier particles of dust—such as silicon, carbon, and iron—attract one another. Some ammonia and methane also are probably drawn into the dust.

Most important for the search for extraterrestrial life, though, is a star's death in a supernova—a spectacular and rare event. When such a titanic explosion occurs, the star spews elements that are key to life as we know it, including sulfur, calcium, phosphorus, iron, and others, into the interstellar medium. From this spewed material, other clouds of dust and gas may form. From there, clumps of matter may begin to draw together, beginning the whole process again.

In December 2000, scientists using a telescope at Kitt Peak Observatory in Arizona detected a simple sugar molecule in a giant cloud of dust and gas from which new stars were forming. This sugar, called glyceraldehyde, is a little like the

Selected in 1958 as the site for a national observatory, today Kitt Peak is home to twenty-two optical telescopes and two radio telescopes, including the largest solar telescope in the world.

sugar you put in your tea. It is an organic substance containing carbon, oxygen, and hydrogen—the same elements found in the building blocks of life. Scientists think this discovery and others like it help show that the chemical precursors to life were formed in clouds long before planets developed around the stars.

Chapter

3

Solar System
E.T.?

If the basic molecules for carbon-based life ride on the backs of common meteorites and grains of dust, couldn't life have begun almost anywhere? Why do some humans think that Earth is so rare and that life has begun only here? Recent discoveries of ancient fossils nearly as old as Earth suggest that life began quickly and easily on Earth. So why couldn't it have happened elsewhere? Why couldn't it have happened on other worlds within our solar system?

Some critics laughingly say that astrobiology is a science without a subject. Since no one has ever found any evidence of life on any other world, what can an astrobiologist study? Astrobiologists, though, see some encouraging signs that life could exist in several other places in our solar system. New evidence gathered by improved telescopes and

Comet West, photographed on March 9, 1976. This photo shows two distinct tails. The blue tail is made up of gases and the broad white tail is made up of microscopic dust particles.

Chris McKay: Ice Diver

Chris McKay is a scientist who is much more comfortable on the frozen, windswept surface of a lake in Antarctica than he is in his crowded, cluttered office at NASA's Ames Research Center in sunny Mountain View, California. Yet he's not the "strong, silent type." He loves to talk about the possibilities of life on Mars, where geologists see evidence of lake beds much like the frozen lakes he has explored.

McKay is a scientist with adventure in his veins. Year after year, he has lowered himself through holes cut in the Antarctic ice to explore the dark regions of mud far below. There he takes samples of mud to be studied. Fossils in this mud tell tales of life-forms that have lived for millions of years, far from the warmth of the Sun. Perhaps these fossils will provide clues about life on other worlds, where extreme cold and darkness prevail.

Christopher McKay in his office.

robot spacecraft encourages researchers such as Chris McKay, an astro-biologist at Ames Research Center (part of the National Aeronautics and Space Administration, or NASA). McKay studies life in extreme environments on Earth. He thinks that if we can understand how life survives at the bottom of a lake in Antarctica that is frozen year-round, then we may have a better idea about where to look for life or fossils of organisms that once existed in extreme environments on other worlds—for example, in rocks beneath the surface of Mars, on Jupiter's icy moon Europa, or on Titan, the big, cloudy moon that orbits Saturn. Some scientists think that even Venus may have once harbored life.

Venus: Too Hot for Comfort!

In the early days of astronomy, Venus seemed the most likely place of all the planets where life might flourish. Venus appears through a telescope to be a lot like our own planet. It has a thick atmosphere that is full of clouds. It has about the same diameter as Earth. It is also our closest neighbor. People imagined lush, green jungles where unusual animals roamed, but no one could actually see the surface of Venus or tell much of anything about it. Thick clouds completely blocked the planet from view, so Venus was a mystery until the second half of the twentieth century.

With radar and space exploration came a new ability to detect the surface through clouds. Even at close range, though, the clouds of Venus are so thick that viewing the surface from an orbiter or space-craft is impossible. So the former Soviet Union sent several spacecraft to land on the surface of Venus. Reaching the surface turned out to be anything but easy, though. The atmosphere of Venus contains large

One of the first color pictures of the surface of Venus, taken by *Venera 13,* in March 1982.

amounts of sulfuric acid, the stuff car batteries contain, which is very hard on spacecraft. The atmospheric pressure at the surface is crushing—ninety to a hundred times greater than what we are used to on Earth. Temperatures are searing, registering as high as 900 degrees Fahrenheit (480 degrees Celsius) at the surface as measured by both U.S. and Soviet spacecraft. So Venus was not very friendly to visitors, and landing a spacecraft took many frustrating tries. Finally, in 1982, the Soviet spacecraft *Venera 13* sent back the first color images of Venus from ground level. For those who may still have been expecting green jungles, forests, lakes, and roaming creatures, the disappointment must have been tremendous. The camera revealed nothing more exciting than a parched slope strewn with rocks and boulders.

In fact, the photos were a little more exciting to look at than that. The color photos from *Venera 13* and its twin, *Venera 14,* make the planet's rocks look yellow-orange, a little like butterscotch, with a few accents of reddish brown. However, we now know that Venus isn't really that color. The reddish hue recorded by the cameras was caused by the planet's thick haze. The thick layers of the atmosphere absorb the shorter wavelengths of light as the sunlight streams through. (In much the same way, we see reddish sunsets on Earth when the Sun sinks low on the horizon and shines through many layers of hazy atmosphere.) The rocky surface of Venus is actually a dark, somber gray.

Beginning in 1990 the U.S. spacecraft *Magellan* orbited Venus and used radar to map the contours of 98 percent of its surface. The result was the most complete map of Venus ever made. The maps show continent-like masses, volcanic cones, and what appear to be vast ocean beds. No water flows there, though. Venus is completely waterless. Its clouds are composed of corrosive acid that can burn off your skin. Its atmosphere is composed primarily of carbon dioxide. As far as anyone knows, no life can exist on Venus. Most scientists think that no life ever did.

Why is Venus so different from Earth? One reason is that Venus's orbit is 30 percent closer to the Sun than is Earth's. A group of scientists created a computer simulation to find out what would happen if Earth were just 10 percent closer to the Sun than it is now. Just this small distance, scientists found, would heat up Earth's oceans. Water vapor and carbon dioxide would evaporate out of the ocean into the air. This change in the atmosphere's chemistry would create an extreme greenhouse effect, that is, radiation from the Sun would pass through the atmosphere to heat Earth's surface. However, the carbon dioxide and water vapor in the atmosphere would not let Earth's infrared radiation, which has longer wavelengths than the Sun's rays, pass from the heated surface back into space. In the same way, the windowpanes of a greenhouse let the Sun's radiation in and then trap the re-radiated infrared rays inside, causing the air inside to remain warmer than the air outside the greenhouse. This effect does exist on Earth, but to a much lesser degree.

On Venus, which is much closer to the Sun, the greenhouse effect is extreme. High temperatures caused by the Sun's heat evaporated carbon dioxide and water vapor into the atmosphere. Radioactive rocks deep beneath the surface of Venus also gave off radiation that heated up the planet's interior and melted the rock inside the planet. This molten rock, or magma, pushed up through the weak spots in the crust. Volcanoes formed that belched even more carbon dioxide into the atmosphere. The thick layer of carbon dioxide trapped the heat and additional incoming solar radiation, and the temperature continued to rise.

Some scientists think that Venus had large quantities of water that boiled away long ago. Close to the surface, spacecraft have found small amounts of free oxygen and tiny bits of water vapor—tiny hints, perhaps, of past oceans of water.

On Earth a delicate balance existed between atmosphere, geology, and living things. The carbon dioxide released from inside the planet through volcanoes quickly became dissolved in the waters of streams, rivers, lakes, and oceans. A mild carbonic acid formed and streamed into the oceans, where its presence, along with other processes, caused carbonate rocks to form on the sea floor. So on our planet, most of the carbon dioxide released into the early atmosphere remained tied up in the oceans and rocks and did not escape into the atmosphere.

As life formed on Earth, plant life began to combine carbon dioxide and water with energy from sunlight to form sugars and starches. This process is known as *photosynthesis,* and it provides energy for most of

Earth's life-forms. Microscopic animals also formed shells made of calcium carbonate (a compound formed from calcium and carbon dioxide). These two processes performed by living organisms removed large quantities of carbon dioxide from our atmosphere and replaced it with oxygen.

Not all the "greenhouse gases" were removed, though. Carbon dioxide, water vapor, and methane gas remained in Earth's atmosphere to continue causing a mild greenhouse effect. This atmospheric "blanket" increased the temperature of the lower atmosphere to about 60° F (16° C). Without this warming, normal temperatures on Earth's surface would plummet below freezing. So in a way, the evolution of life itself has helped make Earth a good place for living things and is closely tied to the history of our planet and its atmosphere.

The Habitable Zone

Based largely on what we see in our own solar system and on logic, astronomers have developed a name for the region surrounding a star in which life could originate and survive. They call this region the habitable zone. This region is the area in which a star's *luminosity* (brightness) produces the right temperature for living things to develop. Water must remain liquid (at least much of the time) without boiling away. In our solar system, three planets once seemed to scientists to be within the habitable zone—Venus, Earth, and Mars. However, we now know that Venus is much too hot to sustain life and has been for a long time. Many scientists estimate that the habitable zone in our solar system starts somewhere outside the orbit of Venus and ends just beyond the orbit of Mars. (Of course, this idea doesn't stop astrobiologists from looking at other locations farther from the Sun.)

Mars: Where Is the Water?

No other place in the solar system has raised more hopes for the discovery of life than Mars. In 1877 Italian astronomer Giovanni Schiaparelli (1835–1910) reported seeing marks on the surface of Mars that he called *canali,* an Italian word meaning "channels." American astronomer Percival Lowell (1855–1916) also saw the marks Schiaparelli had seen. Using his colleague's report as a springboard, Lowell interpreted *canali* to mean "canals"—that is, artificial channels built by intelligent beings. This enthusiastic presentation of Mars as a populated world began to excite both scientists and the public. Astronomers in those days could not turn to the *Hubble Space Telescope* or any of the other spaceborne telescopes we have today that orbit high above Earth's atmosphere. They also had no computers to help record and interpret what they saw from ground-based telescopes. The turbulence of Earth's atmosphere also interferes with images, and optical illusions play tricks on ground-based astronomers' eyes. Before long, many people were convinced that a sophisticated civilization had built massive canals to irrigate the vast Martian desert.

In 1924 radio stations were asked to stop broadcasting at certain times so that astronomers could search for radio signals

This mosaic of Mars was put together using 102 images taken by the *Viking orbiter.*

Taken by *Viking 2*, this photo shows a thin coating of ice on the rocks and soil.

from our Martian neighbors. Nothing came. (This was an interesting precursor to today's searches for radio signals from civilizations orbiting far-off stars, which we discuss in chapter 5.) Finally, NASA's *Mariner* and *Viking* spacecraft took images from just above the Martian surface, and the two *Viking* spacecraft landed there. By then everyone could see that artificial canals did not exist after all. Yet Mars still has a reputation for possessing interesting waterways—even without the elaborate canals that Lowell believed he saw.

Today, planetary geologists are convinced that large quantities of water once moved across the face of Mars. Orbiting spacecraft such as the *Mars Global Surveyor,* currently traveling above the red planet, have shown image after image of channels, gullies, and flow marks that closely resemble landforms created by massive floods on Earth. Others show features that apparently were formed when water gushed out of the Martian surface in sudden spurts. In addition to hints of great rivers and lakes, a large area in the northern polar region may have held an ocean fed by rivers and marked by ice flowing in patterns similar to the patterns caused by ice moving along the ocean floor in Antarctica.

If there was once so much water on Mars, though, where did it all go? The case of water on Mars is a hotly debated topic. Some of the clues seem to contradict each other and don't fit together, and scientists are puzzled.

Because water might once have flowed on Mars in large quantities, some researchers hold out hope for finding microscopic fossils in the soil of former lake beds. Some even think that water might still exist below the ground and that some life-forms could survive the extreme conditions of the cold, arid Martian climate, protected by rocks from ultraviolet radiation and freezing temperatures. They would have to be very different life-forms, though, because the Martian atmosphere is very thin and its climate is rigorous.

Many spacecraft have traveled to nearby Mars. In 1976 twin spacecraft named *Viking 1* and *Viking 2* traveled there and sent landers to photograph the surface and run tests on the Martian soil. One of the *Viking* experiments tested for signs of life but found nothing. In 1997 another spacecraft, called *Mars Pathfinder*, traveled there. It parachuted safely to the surface, bounced to a landing, and opened its petal-like shell to reveal a small rover vehicle the size of a microwave oven. Named *Sojourner*, the vehicle's sturdy wheels carried it across the Martian surface to bump against rocks, scrape samples, and send images to scientists back home.

Mars continues to fascinate people on Earth. As one *Pathfinder* scientist exclaimed as he watched images come in from the surface, "Hey, that looks like New Mexico!" Mars looks a lot like home—especially if home is a cold, dry desert. Long ago, when the atmosphere

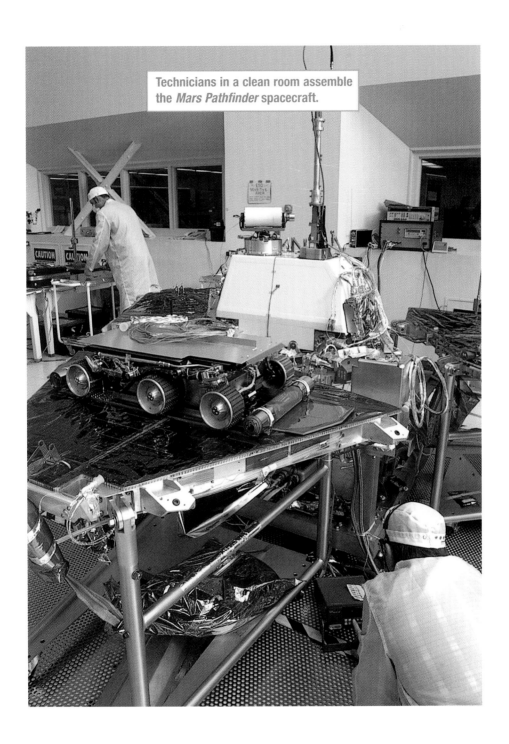

Technicians in a clean room assemble the *Mars Pathfinder* spacecraft.

In 1976 *Viking 1* captured an image that some people imagined was a giant face. (Have you ever seen a cloud that looked like an elephant or a camel?) As happened in the late 1800s with Schiaparelli's *canali,* the enthusiasm of the public grew intense. Planetary geologists knew the

What may once have looked like a huge "face" turns out to be just natural features in this image taken by *Mars Global Surveyor* in 2001. It is just one of thousands of similar buttes, mesas, and ridges in the region.

"face" was just an ordinary mesa, or high plain, like many others nearby. Yet speculation raged in the tabloid newspapers and among some science fiction fans. Some crackpots conceived elaborate stories about how the "face" came to be on the surface of Mars. Perhaps it was a

huge sculpture, a sort of signal to earthlings and others, left by an ancient Martian civilization. Perhaps an advanced civilization from another star system had traveled to Mars and had constructed the face as a sign to earthlings of their presence.

More than twenty years later, in 1998 and again in 2001, the *Mars Global Surveyor (MGS)* captured new images of the same region. Cameras had improved since the *Viking* camera was built, so the *MGS* camera had a much higher resolution. Its images were better focused, capable of showing objects the size of a jet plane. The angle of the Sun in the 1998 photo was different than it was in the earlier photo. The "face" turned out to be nothing but an ordinary arrangement of natural hillocks, ridges, and a large mesa, untouched by anyone, as far as any reasonable person could imagine. No giant sculpture. No signal from another civilization. Just dirt and rock, arranged by the forces of nature. The "face" on Mars was a product of overactive human imagination.

The "face" on Mars is a good example of the principle that the simplest explanation is usually the best one. There's no sign of any past civilization existing anywhere on Mars. And the idea that members of any civilization would travel at least 150 years, probably over a span of generations, to carve a message for us on the surface of a nearby planet is a pretty far-fetched tale. Light and shadow playing across the surface of Mars is a much simpler explanation.

of Mars was thicker, the planet was probably both wetter and warmer. At that time microbial life may have existed. Today, the possibility of life existing on Mars seems unlikely. However, the existence of life on Mars—ancient or present—remains unproved. Many planetary scientists are sure that there was once life on Mars. Finding it, though, is another matter.

Sea Monsters on Europa?

Europa is relatively smooth. In fact, its surface may be the smoothest surface in the solar system. This moon is about the size of our Moon and is the smallest of Jupiter's four moons, which were discovered by the astonomer Galileo. Between the late twentieth and early twenty-first centuries, enormous amounts of new information poured in from a spacecraft named *Galileo* that visited the four moons of Jupiter. As a result we know a lot more about Europa than we did before.

Europa's smooth exterior is what geologists call a young surface, that is, some geologic force covered the impact craters that once existed on Europa's surface. It shows almost no signs of the craters left on most surfaces by the early solar system's period of frequent collisions, the great bombardment.

From *Galileo's* images, we know that an ocean of frozen liquid or slush almost certainly hides beneath Europa's icy crust. Cracks in the moon's icy exterior have probably allowed water or slush to ooze out, flow onto the surface, and then refreeze into a smooth exterior. Even more exciting is the fact that some scientists think Europa may actually hold the chemicals needed for life to begin within that ocean.

What makes scientists think there's an ocean on Europa? By analyzing the light reflected by Europa, scientists have already figured out that the surface is composed of ice. So they've known for some time that, if the interior is warm enough, the underside of that ice could have melted and formed bodies of water. The 1979 *Voyager* images raised some early suspicions, but *Galileo* added three additional clues.

First, *Galileo* showed us a large crater called Pwyll—16 miles (26 kilometers) across—that is very shallow. In fact, the floor of the crater is nearly level with the moon's surface. Yet the meteoroid that caused it hit hard—hard enough to plow into the interior and throw out dark streaks of material. On an object made of solid ice, this impact should have exploded a hole as deep as the Grand Canyon. So Pwyll Crater roused suspicions that fluid material beneath the crust filled the crater almost immediately after it formed.

Second, the images showed large areas composed of chunky-textured blocks of ice. Between these chunks of ice appeared a smooth texture. Researchers think the icy surface has periodically broken apart, exposed the ocean's waters, and then refrozen.

The third clue was that new, icy crust seems to have formed between huge, continent-size plates of ice. These regions resemble regions on Earth's sea floor where lava has broken through. Scientists think that material from Europa's interior is also breaking through here, but on Europa, the interior substance is water or slushy ice, not molten lava.

How could this world, so far away in one of the colder regions of the solar system, have a liquid ocean? No one is sure. A likely cause might be a huge tidal tug from nearby Jupiter. The regions of the moon closest to the center of Jupiter receive a stronger tug of gravity from that planet than regions that are farther away. Europa is so close to massive Jupiter that this tidal force is enormous. The giant planet's spasmodic pull could stretch Europa's insides back and forth. These combined forces could cause Europa's crust to flex and the interior to move and swell from side to side, producing internal heat. In fact, the heat could keep most of the water liquid, despite the frigid surface temperature, forming a giant ocean inside that smooth exterior. Some scientists estimate that this ocean may be ten times deeper than any ocean on Earth.

If an ocean of water (or ice-and-water slush) exists beneath that icy crust, all the necessary elements are very likely present for the formation of life: heat, water, and organic materials (introduced by meteorites). In fact, scientists think that, in the future, researchers may find some simple form of life on Europa. If so, it would be the first time we have ever discovered life anywhere outside Earth's cradling atmosphere. This would potentially be the most dramatic and profound discovery in the history of humankind.

Researchers think that conditions inside Europa might be able to support microorganisms similar to Earth's bacteria. While their size and simplicity may be similar, these living creatures may not be anything like Earth creatures in any other way.

The bright white moon Europa is too far from the Sun to receive much energy from its rays. However, hydrothermal vents deep below the surface of its ocean might provide the needed energy source for life to exist, much as they do for some organisms on Earth.

Titanic Goo

Picture a gooey, dark ocean of hydrocarbons such as methane oozing along a craggy coastline, with orange smog hanging overhead. Tide pools of mushy, brackish-looking gunk lap the shores in the filtered

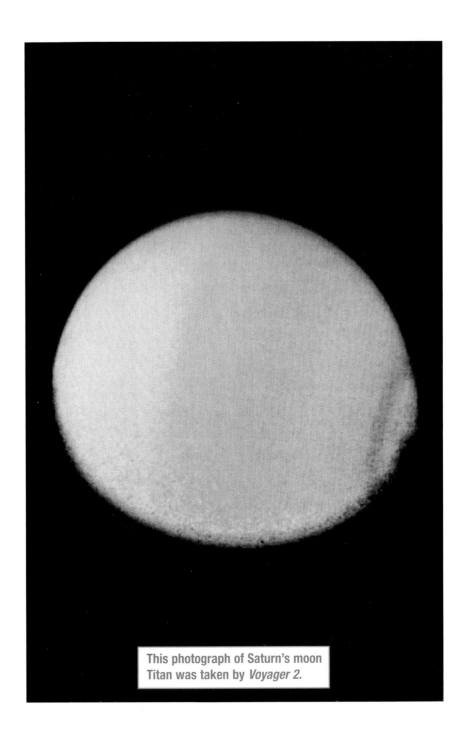

This photograph of Saturn's moon Titan was taken by *Voyager 2*.

light of the faraway Sun and the reflected light of Saturn some 759,200 miles (1,221,850 km) away. This is one scientist's vision of what Titan might be like on the surface. Of course, until more information is obtained, no one can know what it is really like. Are there oceans? Do mountains range across its surface? Or is it fairly smooth like Europa, its surface locked beneath a frozen layer? Does methane rain out of the sky?

Titan is the largest of Saturn's many moons—about one-third larger than our Moon and bigger than either the planet Mercury or the faraway planet Pluto. Of all the moons in the solar system, only Jupiter's moon Ganymede is larger. Titan has attracted the interest of astrobiologists for a long time. Like Venus, it hides beneath a thick, foggy layer of clouds, so we know very little about its surface. Only one spacecraft, *Voyager 2,* has visited Titan, and its stay was brief. It found enough to raise a lot of curiosity, though, and another spacecraft is now on its way to spend more time there. *Cassini-Huygens* is a two-part spacecraft due to arrive at Saturn in 2004. One part, the orbiter *Cassini,* will tour Saturn and its moons. The other, a lander-probe called *Huygens* (after the astronomer who discovered Titan in 1655), is a special visitor to Titan. It will separate from *Cassini* after arrival at Saturn and go its own way. It will then parachute through the atmosphere to the moon's surface. There it will come to rest, take pictures, and report back to scientists on Earth.

Meanwhile, scientists have found out a few facts by studying data from *Voyager 2* and images taken by *Hubble Space Telescope* and ground-based telescopes. Titan's thick atmosphere is composed mostly of nitrogen, as is Earth's. However, the other ingredients of the atmosphere are very different from Earth's current atmosphere. Titan's atmosphere contains traces of hydrocarbons (molecules that combine hydrogen, carbon, and sometimes oxygen in various ways and often exist in the form of oil or natural gas) and other carbon compounds including methane, ethane, acetylene, propane, and so on. That's why scientists envision a rain of methane falling from the atmosphere and dark, oozing oceans of liquid methane.

Titan's atmosphere has lots of the ingredients necessary for life, but it would be completely poisonous to life-forms living on Earth today. *Cassini* will take a close look at Titan's atmosphere and its surface. No one knows exactly where its atmosphere came from. Titan still retains thick, gassy clouds. Could these clouds be composed of primordial gases that date back to the beginning of the big moon's formation in the *solar nebula?* Were they trapped in the icy surface and released slowly over the ages?

Titan's surface conditions raise a lot of questions about the kind of life that could form there. Most astrobiologists think that Titan currently is too cold for life to develop, but could some early precursors to microbial life exist on Titan today? What may happen to Titan in the future if its frigid climate becomes warmed by changes in the Sun? Could organisms begin to form during the Sun's old age? The big moon's similarities to Earth's early stages begin to add up: a primarily nitrogen atmosphere, a "chemistry lab" full of organic molecules, and the possible presence of both oceans and land.

Four or five billion years from now, the temperature on Titan may become more inviting to life. By then our Sun will have reached a late stage of maturity. It will turn red and begin to swell tremendously as it enters the red giant stage. The oceans of Earth will boil away. The Sun's heat will reach out farther and farther into the solar system and reach

Titan, where it may encourage life to form and evolve in the relatively short amount of time left in its life cycle. Long after human life on Earth is gone, a new, though short, chapter of life in the solar system may begin on this big moon of the ringed planet Saturn.

Looking for Life in the Solar System
Vital Statistics

Where	Probability (poor/fair/good/excellent)	Why
MERCURY	Poor	Much too small and close to the Sun—unable to retain an atmosphere. Life would either freeze or fry; no known water, although some frozen water may exist in craters at the poles.
VENUS	Poor	Living organisms almost certainly never developed because high carbon dioxide levels in the atmosphere made it too hot.
EARTH	Excellent	The "pale blue dot," as Carl Sagan called it, is the only home to life known as of yet.
MOON	Poor	Possibly has some water ice, but has been geologically inactive for billions of years and has no atmosphere.
MARS	Fair	Life may have begun here long ago, and exploration may turn up microbe fossils. Some scientists think some microscopic life-forms may exist here now.

Vital Statistics

Where	Probability (poor/fair/good/ excellent)	Why
ASTEROIDS	Poor	Too small, too far from the Sun, no atmosphere.
EUROPA, MOON OF JUPITER	Fair	This frozen world is far from the Sun, yet tidal forces keep its interior warm, and studies show that a liquid ocean probably exists beneath its frozen exterior. Though outside the habitable zone, some life-forms may exist in these waters.
GANYMEDE, MOON OF JUPITER	Fair	May have a liquid ocean, but is probably not as warm as Europa.
TITAN, MOON OF SATURN	Fair	Has atmosphere primarily composed of methane; may have oceans and tide pools of gooey organic matter; probably too cold for life to begin here now, but billions of years from now, life may begin here before the Sun dies.

Chapter 4

Life Beyond Our Solar System

As far as anyone knows, life needs a planet or a moon on which to develop. So one place to begin finding out about life in other solar systems is to look for extrasolar planets. The solar system, you might say, is not the only game in town. By October 2001, astronomers had detected nearly eighty extrasolar planets—objects orbiting stars other than our Sun. All of these planets are too close to their stars or gas giants to be suitable for the development of life as we know it. However, astronomers are confident that the detection of extrasolar planets has just begun. Terrestrial planets—smaller lumps of rock like ours—would of course be more difficult to detect than the massive, gaseous giants that have been found so far.

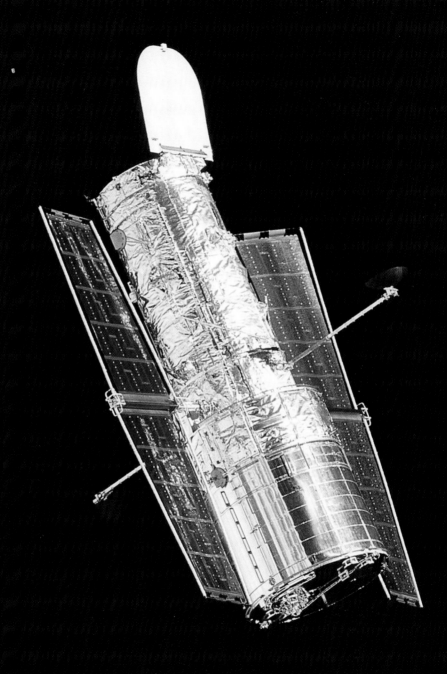

This photo was taken by an astronaut as the Hubble Space Telescope was released from the bay of the space shuttle *Discovery*.

Some researchers think that every star has a planetary system. Planets form from material in a solar nebula—material not swept up into the star itself. They reason that a planetary system fails to form only if the star has consumed all of the available material in the nebula. Estimates for the number of planets in a system range from five to twenty—with the average being about ten. (Our system has nine.) Spectroscopic studies at ground-based observatories, advancements in telescope equipment, the use of CCDs (charge-coupled devices, also used in video cameras and digital cameras), and space telescopes such as the *Hubble Space Telescope* have rapidly increased discoveries. So researchers are excited about what they may find in the near future. Even if these estimates are accurate, the number of planets that could support life is another question.

The Planet Hunt Is On

So far, most of the searches for extrasolar planets are not yet fine-tuned. Therefore, only very large planets have been detected—planets more massive than Jupiter, the largest planet in our solar system. As one astronomer of the Anglo-Australian Observatory in New South Wales, Australia, remarked, "As a result, searches are picking up all the weird, giant planets first." The future, however, looks promising.

Researchers hope to find ways to locate the darker, smaller, rocky planets they think must also be orbiting the same stars as the huge gas giants they have already found. The smaller, Earthlike planets are much more interesting to astrobiologists looking for life elsewhere in the universe because they think life is more likely to exist on a rocky, terrestrial planet.

Until recently, scientists could only guess by a star's wobble that a planet might be located nearby. They couldn't actually see the planet, but they were sure it was there because they could detect its effects on the movement of the star it was orbiting. Now, more advanced telescopes and CCDs may bring much better results. Astronomers have actually caught sight of a few planets crossing the disks of the stars they orbit. When a planet passes between Earth and its star, it blocks a tiny fraction of the star's light for a moment. This is called a *transit*. If three different observations confirm the same event at predictable intervals for the same duration of time and with the same change in brightness, scientists consider the planet's discovery to be confirmed. Planets even smaller than Earth can be detected in this way. Scientists can calculate the size of the planet from the change in brightness of the star. They can also estimate the planet's distance from its star based on the amount of time between transits, and from this they can estimate the planet's temperature.

Astrobiologists think a habitable planet—one on which life might exist—would be thirty to six hundred times less massive than Jupiter. It would also have to orbit within the habitable zone around its star, maintaining an average temperature of about 80° F (27° C).

Looking for Faraway Life

Once scientists have identified a planet of the right size, distance from its star, and temperature, they will begin looking for signs of life. This is difficult, since life is hard to define. However, living things have continual exchanges with their surroundings—specifically, exchanges of matter and energy. In Earth-based biological terms, these exchanges take the form of alimentation (the process of nourishment) and photosynthesis. Living things can also reproduce. In Earth-based terms the key to this process is found in the genetic code of DNA.

As more and more is discovered about the nature of life, scientists will come up with new ways to test for its presence. For some of these, researchers may not need to send a rover to a planet to scoop up soils to test. Methods for remote sensing and knowledge about what to look for is gaining ground rapidly. Researchers are already developing ways to detect what they think of as "signatures of life."

Scientists also look for the presence of factors necessary for life as we know it, such as carbon-based chemistry, the presence of liquids (specifically water), a habitable environment, and so on. They look for planets in the habitable zones of the stars they are searching, and they look for moons within habitable distances of large planets, such as Jupiter and Saturn.

One approach for looking for life is checking for the presence of oxygen—one of the primary signatures of life on our planet. This approach limits consideration to planets that might harbor life like ours, but it is still a good place to begin.

Chapter 5

Looking for Intelligent Life

or humanity, the most intriguing question of all is whether other intelligent civilizations exist elsewhere in the universe. Do we have counterparts on planets revolving around other stars? If so, where are they? If they are out there, how would they communicate with us and what would they say? How would we respond?

Philosophers, storytellers, and science fiction writers have explored this question for hundreds of years, but a good method for searching the skies did not exist until just over forty years ago. In 1960 an *astrophysicist* named Frank Drake established the first scientific search for radio signals from extraterrestrial civilizations. He called it Project Ozma, after the queen of Oz (where Dorothy visited in the film *The Wizard of Oz,* which is based on the book by L. Frank Baum). At the

$$N = R_* f_p n_e f_l f_i f_c L$$

Frank Drake established Project Ozma.

time, Drake was working at the radio astronomy observatory at Green Bank, West Virginia, and he persuaded the director to let him use a radio telescope to begin his search.

The "Water Hole"

Looking for extraterrestrial civilizations can be compared to looking for a needle in a haystack. Where and how do you look, what do you look for? Drake reasoned that a beam of light could easily be absorbed by the clouds of dust that exist in interstellar space. So searching for flashes of light didn't make sense. But radio waves pass easily through all that dust, just as if it weren't there. A technologically advanced civilization might emit radio signals as a consequence of its technology. Since early in the twentieth century, Earth's inhabitants have been broadcasting radio signals in the course of daily living. High-frequency signals, such as FM or television signals, can make their way through our atmosphere and into the great expanse of space. They are traveling even now, as you read this, toward the far reaches of the universe, to be detected and maybe even heard by civilizations, should they exist.

Some civilizations might send radio signals intentionally in an effort to communicate with other civilizations like theirs. Drake and other early researchers listening for signals had little equipment and little time with the telescope to search each month. So they tried to find ways to aim their search at the most likely regions to increase their chances of success. They realized that civilizations might choose to broadcast in a small range of radio frequencies near 1420 megahertz (MHz). It so happens that in this range there is a dip in background noise, so there is less interference from other sources in the universe. So other civilizations might find it a logical region of the spectrum in which to broadcast. Hydrogen, the most widespread element in the universe, radiates at this same frequency. Some researchers who search for signals like to call this range of the spectrum the "water hole," because the dip in background noise makes it a good communication range where civilizations could gather to converse, like office workers who gather at the watercooler. So that's where the researchers began their search.

The Search Begins

On the first night of the search, Drake put on his earphones and pointed the telescope toward a nearby star, Tau Ceti. He listened and listened and listened. Then Tau Ceti sank below the horizon. So Drake turned his telescope toward another nearby star, Epsilon Eridani. Seconds later, he heard a strange sound. A pulsating beat at a rate of eight per second resounded in his earphones. A sudden rush of excitement froze his thoughts for a moment. Then he forced himself to calm down and begin studying the sound. He was a scientist and his job was to observe without bias. Then, suddenly, the sound was gone. Drake never heard the sound again.

What was that sound? The observatory was nestled in an isolated valley of the Allegheny Mountains. Little possibility existed for interference from human-produced radio signals. Afterward, though, Drake found out that the U.S. military was active in the area. He never had any real evidence, but he concluded that an unannounced military exercise was probably the source of his "extraterrestrial" signal. Once again, he realized, the simplest explanation is usually the best one.

Drake's disappointment was keen. Yet, he reasoned, why suppose that a signal would be received within the first hours of observation? Drake still maintained that searching for radio signals from other civilizations made good sense. The following year he organized the first conference to explore methods and issues surrounding this kind of search. The conference went by the name SETI, which stands for the Search for Extraterrestrial Intelligence.

Is Anybody Out There?

For the first SETI conference Frank Drake devised a method for thinking about conducting a search. It is known as the Drake equation, but it isn't really an equation. So many questions surround the search for intelligent civilizations that Drake devised his "equation" to focus on them, one by one. He wanted to determine a way of estimating how many communicating, intelligent civilizations might exist in our galaxy, and his equation is more of a way of thinking about these questions than a specific mathematical formula. It looks like this:

$$N = S^* p_p n_e P_l p_i p_c L$$

This looks scary, but basically, it means that N, on the left, represents the number of intelligent, communicating civilizations in the Milky Way. That number is equal to the product of several factors multiplied together. **N** is the **N**umber of communicating civilizations = the number of **Stars** in the galaxy (**S***) × the **percentage** of those stars that have **planets** (p_p) × the **number** of **environmentally** appropriate planets orbiting each of those stars (n_e) × the **percentage** of those planets that evolve **life** (P_i) × the **percentage** of those planets that evolve **intelligent** life (pi) × the **percentage** of the intelligent life–bearing planets that can **communicate** (p_c) × the **Length** of time (in terms of a fraction of a planet's life) that a communicating civilization may survive (**L**).

The big problem is that no one knows exactly what numbers to use in the equation, because no one really knows the answers to all of the questions Drake posed (see the following table). Still, Drake had outlined a place to begin.

How Many Are Out There?

Drake began by thinking that the development of life requires a planetary system, something like our solar system—with one or more planets that might have become the home of living organisms. Beginning with that idea, each element in the Drake equation stands for

The Drake Equation at Work:
$N = S^* p_p n_e p_l p_i p_c L$

Vital Statistics

Equation Symbol	Explanation	Estimated Number
S^*	**Number of stars:** The number of stars that exist in the Milky Way galaxy	200 billion
p_p	**Planets:** Percentage of those stars that may have planets around them	20%
n_e	**Environment:** Number of planets per star that may be environmentally able to sustain life	3
p_l	**Life:** Of those planets, the percentage that do evolve life	50%
p_i	**Intelligence:** Percentage of planets where life develops that also evolve intelligent life	20%
p_c	**Communication:** Percentage of planets having intelligent life that can communicate	20%
L	**Length of time:** Fraction of the planet's life that a communicating civilization may survive	1/1,000,000th

one of the several factors that influence how many communicating civilizations could exist in our galaxy. The table shows one example of how the equation may be used.

Try calculating an answer by multiplying the number S* by each of the other factors in the column marked Estimated Number: 200,000,000,000 × 0.20 × 3 × 0.50 × 0.20 × 0.20 × (1/1,000,000) = ? Did you come out with 2,400? Do you think there could be 2,400 other communicating civilizations in our galaxy alone? Many SETI researchers think so.

When scientists talk about the Drake equation, they point out that all of the numbers in the Estimated Number column are very tentative, very rough estimates. However, the current estimate for the number of stars in our galaxy is at least 200 billion. Of course, many other galaxies besides the Milky Way also exist—100 billion galaxies or more. Each one of those galaxies may also contain at least 200 to 300 billion stars or more. These may also be "home stars" to many other intelligent civilizations. But let's just talk about our own galaxy for now.

As for the number of planetary systems, as you have already seen, researchers know much more about this number now than they did just a few years ago. New planets are being discovered constantly, and in just a few years a much more accurate estimate will probably be available. Currently, researchers think that nearly all the stars in the Milky Way may have planetary systems! This estimate might be high, though. Try calculating the equation again with an estimate of 5 percent. That makes a big difference! Then there would be only 600 civilizations out there from which to receive communications. Still, that's quite a few.

Most of the other numbers are even more controversial. Consider our solar system. Three of our planets—Venus, Earth, and Mars—look as if they can or could have supported life. Jupiter's moon Europa and Saturn's largest moon, Titan, also are possibilities. Yet Earth is the only one we know of that definitely supports life. So you may want to replace 3 with 1 or even 5, depending on your viewpoint. Try it. When you change the estimates, the outcome changes.

What percent of the planets that *can* support life actually *do* become hosts to living organisms? Some scientists think that the conditions that allowed life to begin on Earth are probably not so rare and that life may not require just those exact conditions. As you know, life on Earth exists in many extreme conditions. Could valid estimates for this factor be as high as 100 percent?

On the other hand, some of the most important chemicals required for life on Earth are actually very rare. Carbon, nitrogen, oxygen, sulfur, phosphorus, calcium, and iron are all among the scarcest in the universe, produced only in supernova explosions. So other researchers are not nearly so optimistic, maintaining that the circumstances on Earth that allowed life to develop are rare. They might put the estimate closer to 0 percent.

Among the planets on which life begins, what percentage develop intelligent life? Again, the range of estimates is broad. No one really knows. Some researchers think that intelligence is such a clear advantage that intelligent life will always develop if it has a chance. Others point to the ancient cockroach. What intelligence does this lowly insect have? Yet it thrives today, almost completely unchanged since it first appeared on Earth more than 320 million years ago. Apparently, a lack of literature and mathematics has had no real negative effect on this insect's survival. So again, estimates range from nearly 100 percent to just above 0 percent.

What about communicating? No one really knows how unique our communication capabilities are. Our abilities are by far the most advanced on Earth and include the means to broadcast our communications using radio waves. How many intelligent civilizations would develop these skills? Since this is basically an unknown quantity, most researchers settle for an estimate of 50 percent.

By the time you get to the last factor, you probably have narrowed down the 200 billion original candidates a lot. One last factor remains in Drake's equation: How long does a planet survive after a communicating civilization has developed there? No one knows. Our own civilization has been "communicating" in the cosmic sense only since the birth of radio and TV. Scientists calculate that Earth and the Sun will probably last a total of about 10 billion years. However, what portion of that time will our civilization survive? Let's be optimistic: If we survive another 10,000 years, the estimate for the last factor would be 1/1,000,000th.

Today, Frank Drake heads the SETI Institute in Mountain View, California, which was founded in 1984. One of the cofounders was Jill Tarter, who directs the Institute's search, Project Phoenix.

Conducting the Search

Today, SETI researchers no longer use earphones, as Drake did in the days of Project Ozma or as Jodie Foster did when she played Ellie Arroway in the movie *Contact*. SETI scientists listen for signals from space using powerful computers that scan for signals and filter out noise and known radio sources. SETI is given small amounts of time

The main character of the 1997 movie *Contact* (as well as the book) was loosely based on a real person: Dr. Jill Tarter. She started out as an engineering student but shifted to astrophysics because she found it more challenging. She was also a talented computer programmer, so as a graduate student at the University of California at Berkeley, she began working on programs for a project called SERENDIP (Search for Extraterrestrial Radio Emissions from Nearby Developed Intelligent Populations). Tarter's curious mind soon began examining the question behind the research: "Are we alone?" She later remarked that she had come to the conclusion that, for her, "it was the most interesting question there could be." She has never stopped asking it. In 1984 she cofounded the nonprofit SETI Institute and served as a principle investigator from 1985 to 1993. In 1997 Tarter was appointed to the Bernard M. Oliver Chair for SETI at the SETI Institute.

Jill Tarter, cofounder of the SETI Institute.

Tarter was a longtime friend of the late world-renowned astronomer Carl Sagan, author of the book *Contact,* a science fiction story about the search for signals from extraterrestrial intelligent communicators. If you read the book or see the movie, you may notice that the book's main character, Ellie Arroway, has a lot in common with Jill Tarter. Like Ellie, Tarter recognizes that she doesn't know everything. If someone came along with hard evidence that a spaceship landed with little green beings aboard, Tarter says she would consider it.

However, she doesn't expect to find E.T.s landing on Earth. The distances between Earth and extrasolar planets are too vast to travel. Tarter does hope that researchers will one day discover a signal from a distant civilization. She is an expert at devising ways to detect potential signals using sophisticated technologies. Tarter believes that scientists may have to search for several generations before they find a signal or conclude that there isn't one out there. Like Ellie, Tarter is a hardworking scientist with vision, determination, and skill. Tarter maintains, though, that "Carl Sagan wrote a book about a woman who does what I do, not about me."

Science at Work: Listening with a Valley

Most radio telescopes look like huge television satellite dishes pointing toward the sky, but not Arecibo. The largest radio telescope in the world is nestled in a natural valley near the town of Arecibo, Puerto Rico. A fence of metal mesh 60 feet (18 meters) high keeps Earth's radio noise from disturbing the big telescope's focus. The main instrument is 1,000 feet (300 m) across. Nearly thirty-nine thousand panels compose its receiving surface. They are supported by a network of steel cables that stretch across the valley. Unlike most radio telescopes, this one does not move. A large platform above the dish gathers signals and transmits them. This platform's instruments can direct the telescope a little bit. Arecibo is a major telescope facility with a varied program of investigation. Scientists generally use the giant dish for more conventional research than SETI. They explore the ionosphere layer of Earth's atmosphere, investigate the surfaces of nearby planets by transmitting and receiving radar signals, and observe radio-transmitting objects in space. Radio astronomy can often detect objects at low temperatures. It is a good method for finding objects not easily detected by other methods of observing, such as optical, infrared, ultraviolet, X-ray, or gamma-ray. Radio astronomy can measure the strength of magnetic fields, while other observing methods cannot. So radio astronomy complements many other kinds of observation.

to use the big radio telescope run by Cornell University at Arecibo, Puerto Rico, and other telescopes.

Frank Drake's first search in 1960 used an 85-foot (26-m) antenna. Today, Project Phoenix continues to target particular stars, much as Drake did with Project Ozma. But much more sophisticated equipment is now available. Beginning in 1995 Phoenix has combined computers and radio telescopes to monitor 28 million channels, or frequencies, at once. Eventually, SETI hopes to monitor two billion channels for each of approximately one thousand nearby stars.

Hello, Neighbor

What about sending a signal? Wouldn't that be a better way to communicate?

Actually, we have sent messages—in addition, that is, to roughly sixty years of daily radio transmissions and television programs. One effort was made on November 16, 1974, by SETI to send a communication to listeners in space. SETI scientists used the Arecibo Observatory to broadcast a message in binary code—the two-digit, on-off code used by computers. A technological civilization, they reasoned, would understand binary code because it is a common, universal system that reflects

The Arecibo radio telescope, located in Puerto Rico, is the largest radio telescope in the world. It can send and receive signals to examine planets and asteroids. It also analyzes Earth's upper atmosphere.

the way physics works throughout the universe. The message information included numeric information that is important to life as we know it and to human civilization. They sent the numbers 1 through 10; the atomic numbers of hydrogen, carbon, nitrogen, oxygen, and phosphorous (elements found throughout the universe and important to life on Earth); a code representing DNA and its shape; a simple diagram of a human being; Earth's population and position in the solar system; and a schematic diagram of Arecibo. The target was a globular cluster of stars twenty-five thousand light-years away in the constellation M13 Hercules. Chances are good that we'll never receive a reply, even if the message gets there. The answer would take another twenty-five thousand years to return, since nothing in the universe travels faster than light.

Two more messages were sent three years later. In 1977 two U.S. interplanetary spacecraft, *Voyager 1* and *Voyager 2,* were launched to visit Jupiter and the outer solar system. After traveling through the outer solar system, these two spacecraft have just kept on going. They were both still in contact with NASA in December 2000. Both have enough momentum and fuel to last until about 2020, and both are now speeding through interstellar space.

Someday—though the likelihood is remote—another civilization could possibly find one of these spacecraft. So NASA engineers attached a plaque—actually, a gold-plated phonograph record—to each spacecraft's exterior. Each record contains encoded pictures of Earth and of a male and female human being. It also conveys greetings in fifty-four languages, a selection of sounds from Earth, and ninety minutes of various types of music. (Today, graphics and movies could have been added in CD or DVD format, but the two *Voyager* spacecraft began their voyages too long ago for that.) As these two spacecraft travel toward very distant places, they carry these messages with about as much, or as little, hope of discovery as two stoppered glass bottles carrying messages on the high seas.

Of course, if contact did take place, it would happen hundreds to thousands of years from now. That's how long it would take for either spacecraft to reach any stars around which civilizations could exist that might understand, or even hear, any of the material on the records.

Some people worry about telling "aliens" too much. What if civilizations on other worlds aren't friendly? Hollywood movies and science fiction tales are filled with accounts of attacks by aliens. Of course, friendlier tales have also been told. However, neither friend nor foe has ever replied—the distances are far too vast.

Delivery Time

In fact, this extreme time lag is one of the frustrations of SETI's search. Suppose we do pick up a signal. The speed of light (and all portions of the electromagnetic spectrum) is the fastest that anything in the universe can travel. Radio waves are also part of the *electromagnetic spectrum*, so that's their speed of travel, too. So a signal received from another solar system today had to begin its journey thousands of years ago. By the time we find out about it, the civilization could have disappeared. So searching for extraterrestrial intelligence is more like looking for a good history book or a letter in a time capsule than it is like making a telephone call.

There is also no reason to think that the lack of signals is evidence that no intelligent, communicating life exists anywhere else in the universe. It may be there today, and it may even be sending out signals loudly and clearly. Yet, because of the distances between us, we cannot hear them. All we can hear is the great silence that existed millions of years ago. Today's clamor will take millions of years to reach our solar system. Other planets that could harbor life may also exist today, but we cannot see them as they are at this time. We can only detect their pasts.

Chapter 6

What If?

If we can't communicate, then why are we searching? We have been "listening" for intelligent extraterrestrial signals for more than forty years with no success. Even if we were to receive a message, our answer is unlikely to be heard. Two-way communication cannot take place. So what do we gain by our search?

The answer is knowledge. If we do receive a signal, we would know that we are not alone. Then we would know that we are not the only advanced, intelligent life in the universe. We might discover that we are part of a vast community of beings who have found different ways to survive in the universe. We may learn something about how other civilizations have organized, what they have found out about the universe, and what practical or theoretical solutions they may have found for universal problems. Intellectually, we know that Earth is not the center of the universe. However, if SETI succeeds in finding a signal from another civilization, we would understand more about our role in the universe.

SETI scientists think their search deserves at least another twenty years, or even more, to find the answer to the question "Are we alone?"

If no evidence of extraterrestrial intelligence is found, we might conclude that we are unique after all. Of course, we will never know this as absolute fact, but if the odds begin to show that we are probably the only intelligent beings in the universe, that, too, will have an effect. Then we would realize the great fragility of our legacy, and we might recognize the vast responsibility we have for perpetuating the existence of intelligent life. What if no other civilization exists that has developed art, music, poetry, literature, and science? Humanity would be solely responsible for continuing everything that we have begun. This would be an enormous, even frightening, responsibility.

The search for life on other worlds also goes beyond SETI, as you have seen. It includes the exploration of other worlds in our solar system and the study of planets orbiting other stars. It also includes exploring the nature of biology in the most universal, general sense. The more we explore, the more we learn about the universe and how it works. In the process, we may discover that life at various stages may be found in many different places.

NASA has begun a twenty-year project called the Origins Program. It spans many areas of inquiry, combining the talents of biologists, chemists, physicists, astronomers, and many others. It also takes advantage

These dish antennae make up a part of the Very Large Array (VLA) near Socorro, New Mexico. The VLA is the world's largest radio telescope array, consisting of twenty-seven dishes.

of important breakthroughs in science and technology that open up new ways of searching and investigating. Sophisticated telescopes and technologies will join the effort aimed at finding out more about how and where life began.

The current generation and the next have the privilege of meeting the challenges of these quests, thanks to advances never before available. Maybe the early twenty-first century will be remembered as the epoch in which we discovered that we are not alone.

Or maybe we will begin to know how unique we humans are in the universe. In any case, as we explore more and more of the universe, we are certain to see ever more clearly the great beauty of the oasis we call Earth.

Key Searches for Life on Other Worlds

Vital Statistics

Name of Search	Year Begun	About the Search
PROJECT OZMA	1960	First search for radio signals from intelligent civilizations on other worlds.
VIKING LANDERS	1976	Two landing craft touch down on the surface of Mars and run experiments intended to test for evidence of life. No positive results are found (NASA).
SETI INSTITUTE	1984	SETI project search begins; in 1985 NASA funding begins.
PROJECT PHOENIX	1993	Federal funding of SETI project ends; Project Phoenix continues the SETI Institute's search using private funding and shared time on astronomy observatories.
MARS GLOBAL SURVEYOR	1996	Spacecraft launched to orbit Mars and map its surface; in 1999 it begins mapping and finds evidence that water may currently exist (NASA).
DARWIN PROJECT	1996	Studies begin for *Darwin* spacecraft to use special instruments to search for chemical signs of life on alien, Earthlike planets; scheduled to launch in 2010 (ESA).

Vital Statistics

Name of Search	Year Begun	About the Search
Mars Pathfinder/ Sojourner	1997	Spacecraft lands on Mars to study the surface; *Pathfinder* rover examines rocks up close (NASA).
Huygens Probe	1997	Launched with Cassini-Huygens mission to Saturn and Titan (NASA/ESA) to examine Titan's atmosphere and surface; planned arrival is 2004.
Mars Odyssey	2001	Orbiter arrives at Mars to study planet's climate and geologic history, including a search for water and evidence of life-sustaining environments (NASA).

Life on Other Worlds: A Timeline

4th century B.C. — Epicurus, a Greek philosopher, puts forth the idea that Earth is only part of the infinite universe; he envisions the existence of many other worlds with many different kinds of inhabitants.

56 B.C. — Lucretius, a Roman philosopher and poet, speculates that life exists in other parts of the cosmos.

A.D. 1543 — Nicolaus Copernicus publishes *On the Revolutions of the Heavenly Spheres,* the first recognition that the Sun, not Earth, is at the center of the solar system.

1600 — Giordano Bruno is burned at the stake for his belief that there are many worlds, among other beliefs.

1953 — Experiments by Stanley Lloyd Miller and Harold Clayton Urey demonstrate one way in which organic material may have been produced naturally in the environment of early Earth.

1960 — Project Ozma begins; it is the first search for extraterrestrial intelligence to use radio astronomy.

1961 — Frank Drake devises the "Drake equation" to estimate the number of communicating civilizations that may exist in the Milky Way.

1967 — U.S. *Mariner 5* and Soviet *Venera 4* probes to Venus report such high temperatures that scientists conclude that life is not possible on this planet.

1976 — *Viking 1* and *Viking 2* landers set down on the surface of Mars and test for evidence of the presence of life in the Martian soil, with no positive results.

1977 — Vents of very hot water are found deep in the Atlantic Ocean.

1982 — The International Astronomical Union sets up a commission, "Bioastronomy, the search for extraterrestrial life."

Voyager flies by Titan for the first close look at Saturn's biggest moon, the only moon shrouded by a thick, cloudy atmosphere.

1984 — The SETI Institute is founded.

1985	NASA grants funds for SETI Institute's targeted search.
1993	Federal funding for SETI ends.
1994	The SETI Institute establishes the privately funded Project Phoenix to continue the search.
1995	European Space Agency (ESA) launches the Infrared Space Observatory (ISO), which explores interstellar space for three years and finds mineral grains from which an Earthlike planet might form and water and carbon compounds that could form the building blocks of life.
	Swiss astronomers Michel Mayor and Didier Queloz annouunce that they detect a a planet orbiting star 51Pegasi, the first planet discovered orbiting a solar-type star outside our solar system. The planet, probably a gas giant, is named 51 Pegasi b.
1996	ESA begins to study possibilities for a spacecraft called *Darwin*, which would use special instruments to search for chemical signs of life on alien, Earthlike planets.

NASA scientists announce they have found signs of life in a Martian meteorite, ALH84001; their discovery remains controversial and unconfirmed.

The first firm evidence of a planet outside our solar system is discovered.

2000 — *Mars Polar Lander* reaches Mars carrying probes to search the soil for water; however, communication is lost and no data is received.

2001 — As of October 15, the number of discovered extrasolar planets reported is nearly eighty.

2003 — ESA's *Mars Express* is to land on Mars to look for water; the spacecraft carries the *Beagle 2* lander to look for signs of methane—a possible signal of the presence of persistent life.

NASA and ESA's *Rosetta* is to be launched to study the comet Wirtanen and its chemistry; mission plans include a lander to examine the comet's surface and coma possibly providing insights about the origins of our solar system.

2004 — Allen Telescope Array is to become partially operational.

ESA's *Huygens* probe is to arrive at Saturn and parachute through the atmosphere of Titan, Saturn's largest moon, which may be frozen in a stage similar to early stages of chemistry on Earth, which led to the origins of life on our planet.

2005 — Allen Telescope Array is to begin full operation in a twenty-four-hour, seven-day-a-week search for signals from extraterrestrial intelligent life.

2009 — NASA's Space Interferometry Mission is due to launch, continuing the search for stars with planets.

2012 — NASA's *Terrestrial Planet Finder* is due to launch four advanced telescopes flying in formation to form a giant telescope and look for extrasolar planets.

accretion—the process of growing larger by accumulation of particles or pieces

amino acid—a type of organic molecule, especially one of more than twenty that combine to form proteins

asteroid—a remnant from the formation of the solar system that orbits the Sun

asteroid belt—region between Mars and Jupiter where most asteroids orbit

astrobiologist—a scientist who studies either the origins and environments of life or the possibility of life on other worlds

astrophysicist—a scientist who studies the physical properties and dynamic processes of celestial bodies and phenomena

atmosphere—the gases that surround an object in space, such as the Sun, a planet, or a moon

axis—the imaginary line running from pole to pole through a planet's center. A planet spins, or rotates, along its axis.

carbonaceous chondrites—a class of very old stony meteorites containing chondrules as well as organic compounds (compounds including carbon and oxygen)

comet—a small ball of rock and ice that orbits the Sun. When a comet approaches the Sun, some of the ice melts and releases gases. These gases form a tail on the side of the comet away from the Sun.

composition—what something, such as the Sun, a star, or a planet, is made of

cycle—a series of patterns or events that repeats on a regular schedule

density—how much of a substance exists in a given volume; the amount of mass in a given volume of a particular substance. Each material has a specific density—so no matter how much you have, it always has the same density.

deoxyribonucleic acid (DNA)—a nucleic acid contained in a living cell and responsible for carrying the code that determines individual hereditary characteristics; capable of replicating itself and synthesizing RNA (ribonucleic acid)

diameter—the distance in a straight line measured from a surface through the center to the opposite surface of a sphere, such as the Sun or a planet

electromagnetic spectrum—the full range of the waves and frequencies of electromagnetic radiation. Radio and infrared rays, at one end of the spectrum, have very long wavelengths and are invisible to human eyes. Visible light is about in the middle. At the other end of the spectrum are types of radiation with such short wavelengths that they are invisible to humans, including ultraviolet (UV) waves, X rays, and gamma rays.

eukaryotic—describes an organism (a eukaryote) composed of cells having nuclei. All organisms having more than one cell—including human beings—are eukaryotes.

galaxy—one of the many large-scale groups of billions of loosely associated stars, dust, and gases that make up the universe

gravity—the force that pulls things toward the center of a large object in space, such as a star, planet, or moon; the attraction exerted by an object with mass. The gravity of the Moon creates the tides on Earth; Jupiter's gravity influences its moons and all nearby objects, including asteroids in the asteroid belt; gravity keeps Earth in orbit around the Sun.

hypothesis (pl. hypotheses)—an explanation of a set of facts that can be tested; the basis for a theory *interstellar*—from or in the regions of space between or among the stars (from Latin *inter,* "between or among," and Latin *stella,* "star")

light-year—the distance light travels in one year, about 5.88 trillion miles (9.46 trillion km)

luminosity—a star's brightness

mass—the amount of material a body contains, measured in grams (g) or kilograms (kg)

metabolism—all the chemical processes and reactions that take place in a living organism

meteorite—a chunk of a rock from space that has struck the surface of a planet or moon

nuclear fusion—the reaction that takes place when light atomic nuclei combine to form a heavier nucleus with the release of energy

nucleotides—complex organic molecules that number among the building blocks of life; now known to be the main ingredients of DNA and RNA

nucleus, (pl. nuclei)—the central portion of an atom; composed of a proton, or protons and neutrons; carries a positive charge and contains nearly all of the atom's mass

orbit—the path an object, such as a planet, travels as it revolves around another body, such as the Sun

organic—relating to living organisms; in chemistry, relating to certain carbon compounds (See *organic molecule*)

organic molecule—the smallest possible unit of a class of compounds containing carbon, capable of forming long chains of carbon molecules. A molecule is a group of atoms held together by chemical forces; organic molecules form the basis for all known life.

photon—the smallest quantity of electromagnetic energy, a "piece of light"; has no mass, no charge, and an unknown lifetime

photosynthesis—the process by which plants use the energy of sunlight to produce organic compounds (sugar) from carbon dioxide and water and release oxygen. Plants use the sugar as food, and the oxygen is a waste product of the process.

planetesimal—one of many small bodies that orbited the infant Sun and later accreted, or combined, to form larger planets and moons *prokaryotic*—describes an organism (a prokaryote) composed of cells having no nucleus. Prokaryotes are the most primitive life-forms; bacteria are prokaryotes.

protostar—a very young star at the beginning of its formation

revolution—one complete tour in an orbit around the Sun

revolve—to move in a path, or orbit, around another object. Earth revolves around the Sun, making a complete trip in one year.

ribonucleic acid (RNA)—one of the building blocks of life, important to transmission of genetic information and the manufacture of protein by living cells

rotate—to turn or spin around a central point

rotation—one complete turn of an object in space on its axis

solar nebula—a cloud of gas and dust from which the Sun and the planets were formed

transit—the journey taken by an object as it seems to travel across the disk of a bright object it is orbiting (like an eclipse). For example, a planet's transit occurs when it passes between Earth and the planet's star.

The news from space changes fast, so it's always a good idea to check the copyright date on books, CD-ROMs, and videotapes to make sure that you are getting up-to-date information. Good places to look for current information from NASA are U.S. government depository libraries. There are several in each state.

Books

Campbell, Ann Jeanette. *The New York Public Library Amazing Space: A Book of Answers for Kids.* New York: John Wiley & Sons, 1997.

Hartmann, William K., and Don Miller. *The Grand Tour: A Traveler's Guide to the Solar System.* New York: Workman Publishing, 1993.

Jefferis, David. *Alien Lifesearch: Quest for Extraterrestrial Organisms.* New York: Crabtree Publishing Co., 1999.

Vogt, Gregory L. *The Solar System: Facts and Exploration.* Scientific American Sourcebooks. New York: Twenty-First Century Books, 1995.

CD-ROM

Beyond Planet Earth
Discovery Channel School
P.O. Box 970
Oxon Hill, MD 20750-0970
For the Macintosh and PC (DOS, Windows, OS2), from the Discovery Channel School Multimedia, this is an interactive journey to the planets and moons, including Venus, Mars, Europa, and Titan. It includes video from NASA and *Voyager* missions and more than two hundred photographs.

Video

Discover Magazine: Solar System
Discovery Channel School
P.O. Box 970
Oxon Hill, MD 20750-0970

Organizations and Websites

Many of the websites listed below are NASA sites, with links to many other interesting sources of information about the origins of life, life and its environments, and the search for extraterrestrial life. You can also sign up to receive NASA news on many subjects via e-mail.

Antarctica: Looking for Life

http://www.pbs.org/wnet/nature/antarctica/looking.html

This page examines the existence of life in the extreme conditions of Antarctica, and what these amazingly hardy organisms show about the nature of life and the possibilities of life on other worlds.

The Astronomical Society of the Pacific

http://www.aspsky.org/

390 Ashton Avenue
San Francisco, CA 94112

This organization is devoted to expanding knowledge about the universe and astronomy.

The Astronomy Café

http://www.theastronomycafe.net

This site answers questions and offers news and articles relating to astronomy and space by astronomer and NASA scientist Sten Odenwald.

NASA Ancient Life on Mars

http://spaceflight.nasa.gov/mars/science/ancient/index.html

This site offers capsule information about the search for evidence of ancient primitive life on Mars and the state of existing evidence, and includes answers to frequently asked questions (FAQs).

NASA Ask a Space Scientist

http://image.gsfc.nasa.gov/poetry/ask/askmag.html#list

This interactive page is where NASA scientists answer your questions about astronomy, space, and space missions. It also has archives and fact sheets.

NASA Astrobiology Institute
http://nai.arc.nasa.gov/
NASA's Astrobiology Institute offers this interactive page filled with the latest news about understanding life on Earth, including extreme life, the origins of life, and the search for life on other worlds. It includes an easy-to-understand tour of hydrothermal vents, many links to related sites, and an "Ask an Astrobiologist" service.

NASA Newsroom
http://www.nasa.gov/newsinfo/newsroom.html
Here, you'll find NASA's latest press releases, status reports, and fact sheets. The site includes a NASA news archive for past reports and a search button for the NASA Web. It also allows you to sign up for e-mail versions of all NASA press releases.

NASA Origins Program
http://origins.jpl.nasa.gov
The Origins Program seeks to answer two basic questions: "Where did we come from?" and "Are we alone?" In other words, how did everything begin, including the universe, the solar system, and life on Earth? This page provides up-to-date information about progress scientists are making toward answering these questions.

The Nine Planets: A Multimedia Tour of the Solar System

http://www.seds.org/nineplanets/nineplanets/nineplanets.html

This site, created by the Students for the Exploration and Development of Space at the University of Arizona, includes excellent material on our solar system.

Ocean Planet: Recently Revealed

http://seawifs.gsfc.nasa.gov/OCEAN_PLANET/HTML/oceanography_re cently_revealed1.html

This page at the Smithsonian Institution's Ocean Planet website offers a discussion of the 1977 discovery of life near hydrothermal vents on the ocean floor.

Planetary Missions

http://nssdc.gsfc.nasa.gov/planetary/projects.html

This page of NASA links to all of current and past missions is a one-stop shopping center to a wealth of information.

The Planetary Society

http://www.planetary.org

65 North Catalina Avenue

Pasadena, CA 91106-2301

This organization is devoted to the development of new planetary missions and increasing knowledge about the planets and solar system. The Planetary Society publishes a magazine containing news and updates.

The SETI Institute Online

http://www.seti-inst.edu

The SETI (Search for Extraterrestrial Intelligence) Institute's website includes information about current SETI research, answers to frequently asked questions (FAQs), and plans for future improvements in the search.

Sky Online

http://www.skypub.com

This website for *Sky and Telescope* magazine and other publications of Sky Publishing Corporation has a good weekly news section on general space and astronomy news. The site also contains many good tips for amateur astronomers, as well as a nice selection of links. A list of science museums, planetariums, and astronomy clubs organized by state helps locate nearby places to visit as well.

Solar and Heliospheric Observatory (SOHO) Mission

http://sohowww.nascom.nasa.gov

This is the official site of the SOHO mission, a joint ESA/NASA mission to study the Sun's internal structure.

University of California Planet Search Project

http://exoplanets.org

Check here for the latest news on extrasolar planets, as well as the search for planets like our own.

Welcome to the Planets

http://pds.jpl.nasa.gov/planets/

This tour of the solar system, which includes lots of pictures and information was created by the California Institute of Technology for NASA/Jet Propulsion Laboratory.

Windows to the Universe

http://www.windows.ucar.edu

This NASA site, developed by the University of Michigan, includes sections on "Our Planet," "Our Solar System," "Space Missions," and "Kids' Space." Choose from presentation levels of beginner, intermediate, and advanced. To begin exploring, go to the URL above and choose "Enter the Site."

Bold numbers indicate illustrations.

About the Authors

Ray Spangenburg and **Kit Moser** write together about science and technology. This husband-and-wife writing team has written forty-six books and more than one hundred articles. Their works include a five-book series on the history of science and a series on space exploration and astronomy. Their writing has taken them on some great adventures. They have flown on NASA's Kuiper Airborne Observatory (a large plane carrying a telescope). They have also visited the Deep Space Network in the Mojave Desert, where signals from spacecraft are collected. They have even flown in zero gravity on an experimental NASA flight. Ray and Kit write in Carmichael, California, where they live with their Boston terrier, F. Scott Fitz.